UNBREAKABLE:

GRACEY'S REDEMPTION

BY

DIANA CARTER

UNBREAKABLE:

GRACEY'S REDEMPTION

DIANA CARTER

P.O. Box 300795
Drayton Plaines, MI 48330
ldtpllc@gmail.com

Unbreakable: Gracie's Redemption

Romance/Family Drama/Relationships

All Rights Reserved

Copyright © 2020 by Diana Carter

    This book is a work of fiction. Names, characters, places, and incidents are the product of the author's imagination or are used fictitiously. Any resemblance to actual events, locales, or persons, living or dead, is coincidental

    This book may not be reproduced, transmitted, or stored in whole or in part by any means, including graphic, electronic, or mechanical without the express written consent of the publisher except in the case of brief quotations embodied in critical articles and reviews.

LET'S DO THIS PUBLISHING, LLC
P.O. Box 300795
Drayton Plaines, MI 48330

ISBN 13: 9781733154871

All Rights Reserved

PRINTED IN THE UNITED STATES OF AMERICA

OTHER BOOKS WRITTEN BY DIANA CARTER

BROKEN PROMISES SERIES

Shattered Dreams
When Shattered Dreams Become Reality
Shattered Dreams The Final Chapter
In The Name of Justice: The Erica Blackstone Chronicles

DARK REVENGE SERIES

The Trey Taylor Story
When Time Runs Out: Tara's Quest for Vengeance
TJ The Forgotten Brother

THE SISTER FACTOR SERIES

Diamond's Fight for Justice
Dior's Darlings Daycare
Kristina's Kozy Korner
Krystal's House of Secrets
Never a Dull Moment: The Nick Jr. Story

UNBREAKABLE SERIES

Unbreakable: When Two Hearts Become One
Unbreakable Deux

THE MAKING OF A LEGEND SERIES

Neek's Rise to Fame
Desi's Drive to Survive

SINGLE TITLE

The Candidate: The Race to the Top

Dedication

This book is dedicated to a person that has brought so much joy into my life even though she has only been around a few months my youngest granddaughter, Lyanna Carmen Carter. Lyanna gives me the inspiration to moved forward and persevere through the tough times. The light that shines when she smiles brightens the entire room. Looking down at the many faces she portrays keeps me busy thinking what each look means. I thank God everyday for bringing her into my life. Her journey here wasn't easy but well worth the wait.

Acknowledgements

Wow is all I can say about the penning of the third book in the romance series **Unbreakable**. **Unbreakable: Gracey's Redemption** is a testimonial that if you want to change your life it's possible. The first step to change is wanting it more than anything else. The uphill battle may not be easy but rewarding. I praise God for giving me the dedication and encouragement to pen my eighteen book. Never in a million years would I have thought this would be possible. My thoughts when I first started writing was if I could get this one book published, I would be happy. The words kept coming that turned into ideas that finally turned into series that can be enjoyed by the young and old.

This year has brought the most unusual and unsettling times we have ever faced. Wondering if we would ever get back to normal has forced this country to accept a new normal. I would like to acknowledge a special young man that has face some harsh times in his young life that forced him to grow up faster than expected my oldest grandson, Earnest Burrell. Earnest life hasn't been easy, but he is staying strong not only for himself but to be a good role model for his younger siblings. His passions drive him to move forward and not look back. I love the young man you have become. Keep moving forward to making all your dreams a reality.

God's blessing,
Diana Carter

Unbreakable: Gracey's Redemption

Chapter One

Gracey's looked around her new condo. She couldn't believe this was her place. She thought she would never move out of her parents' house. Striking out on her own made her feel complete for the first time in her life. The demons she had to fight while she was in rehab nearly destroyed her life. She still didn't have a relationship with her twin brother, Greg. She single-handed destroyed Greg's relationship with the most important woman in his life, his ex-wife London. She also didn't have a relationship with her younger brother, Glenn but that didn't concern her because they never gotten along anyways.

Gracey thought about Greg a lot while she was in rehab. Knowing that her actions was the direct cause of his annulment from London still ate away at her. It took her months to get to this way of thinking. When she was first admitted into rehab nine months ago, she blamed all her problems on Greg's relationship with London. Greg was always there to clean up her messes until he met London. Gracey now see that is why she resented London so much.

Heading to the den in her new place, Gracey reflected on the time when she was first admitted into rehab. She felt isolated and alone. The one person she could count on beside Greg was her Uncle Grant (her dad's twin brother), that is until he left her in the wind too when guilt took over after he covered up her part in the hit-and-run of London's twin brother Logan and sister-in-law, Naomi. At first her Uncle Grant was one hundred percent on her side to get London out of Greg's life. They conspired non-stop until the hit-and-run eventually torn their family apart.

Gracey was so angry at her parents, Greg, and Uncle Grant that it was nearly a month before she consented to see them. She couldn't deal with the fact that even after she left rehab, she would still be on probation for causing the accident. She received two years' probation and forced commitment to the treatment center instead of jail time. That was the last straw for London. She annulled her marriage to Greg once she found out none of his family members were going to pay for almost killing her brother, sister-in-law, and their children.

Greg and London were newlyweds. Their marriage couldn't survive the part Greg played in covering up Gracey's crime. It was bad timing because London was four and half months pregnant. Losing his wife and child nearly destroyed Greg, but Gracey wasn't aware just how much she destroyed her brother's life until that first visit, she received from her parents and uncle. They sat in the large visiting room in the farthest corner of the room so they could have a little privacy. Gracey started the conversation.

"So, let me have it."

"This is all you have to say after keeping us away for a month?" Gloria asked her daughter.

"Where is Greg?" Gracey asked.

"We haven't seen much of him since you left." Greg Sr answered his daughter.

"What's his problem. He was the only one I had on my visitor's list, but he never bothered to come see me.

"What did you expect, Gracey. You single handily tore his whole world apart."

"Don't get so upset honey." Gloria said to her husband.

"Why are you so quiet Uncle Grant?" Gracey asked.

"I've had time to think. What we did was horrible. I'm finding it hard to deal with my decisions." Grant answered.

"Stop being such a softie. That wife of his is the one that tore Greg's life apart. I told him she was no good for him." Gracey continued.

"Are you listening to yourself. This is not London's fault. For your information she is no longer his wife." Gloria said.

Gracey stood and started dancing in the small space between her and her family. "That is the best news I've had since being locked up in this joint."

"Gracey your brother is devasted. London had their marriage annulled." Gloria continued.

"So, he will bounce back. He always does. This time I hope he choose someone that is worthy of our family."

"London is pregnant, Gracey. Greg has not only lost his wife, but also his unborn child." Grant said sadly.

"With her background there would be no problem with our family getting custody of that child."

"That is not what Greg wants, Gracey. He told London that he would give her some space and let her decide about visitation and custody of their child." Greg Sr explained.

"Why is he being so soft. I need to speak to him to knock some sense into his head." Gracey said angrily.

"You are the last person Greg wants to see right now, Gracey. Whenever your name comes up, he shuts down." Gloria said. She was so ready to leave. She could see her daughter was still selfish and self-centered.

"Why is everyone making me out to be the bad guy here. I'm not the only one that wanted London out of Greg's life." Gracey said rolling her eyes at her uncle.

"I was wrong, Gracey and so were you to do all the things we did to London." Grant said taking up for himself.

"You guys could leave if that is the only reason you came up here was to try to make me feel bad."

"We will leave, Gracey, but you need to think about what you did. We were all wrong for trying to protect you from the hit-and-run." Greg Sr said.

"I have nothing else to say. Tell Greg, I'll be waiting on him. Tell that other son of yours he shouldn't bothered to come because he is not only my visitor's list." Gracey got up and walked away from her family.

Coming back to the present, Gracey realize she was hungry. While she was making herself a snack she wondered when she would see Greg again. He never came to see her in the six months she was in rehab and he made sure every time he visited their parents for the three months after she came home from rehab she wasn't there. The attitude she had on the first visit with her family was most definitely not the way she felt about the situation today. She had come to accept responsibility for her actions and couldn't wait to try to make it up to everyone for what she did when she was sick.

For the foreseeable future she was still in therapy once a week as an outpatient. She realized she has come a long way, but she had so much farther to go to become healthy. Eventually she would have to face Greg, London, Logan, Naomi, and the boys that her Uncle Grant forced to take the blame for her actions. She didn't know how to make this happened because none of these people wanted anything to do with her, but she would try. She wanted to have a relationship with her family again, especially her beautiful niece Rennie. Greg and London's baby girl was three months old now and from the pictures at her parents house she was a real sweetheart. Rennie's full name was Lorena Gordon Lewis.

Cleaning up her mess, Gracey decided to get ready for her first out-patient therapy appointment since moving into her new place. She had a feeling the only people that would be visiting her would be her parents. Sadly, her Uncle Grant died of a massive heart attack two months before she was released from rehab. Since the wounds were still open, she was not allowed to go to his funeral. Her parents said it would be too hard on the rest of her family for her to be there. As she headed out the door, she wondered how many more family events she would have to miss.

Unbreakable: Gracey's Redemption

Chapter Two

Gracey sat in the waiting room a little frustrated. She knew she would be in for a battle with Dr. Burbank. She was ready to move full speed with her life, but the good doctor said it was too soon for her to approach the people she hurt. It's been three months so Gracey was tired of waiting. Today she planned on asking Dr. Burbank about Greg.

Gracey felt this would be a lot easier if she could just meet with Greg. The last time she saw her twin brother was the night before she was committed to rehab. London had just found out about the hit-and-run coverup by Greg's family. Greg was a mess. His hair was tossed from running his fingers through it unconsciously so many times. His clothes looked like he had slept in them. Greg entered the family room where Gracey, their parents, Uncle Grant, and younger brother Glenn were sitting. Gracey stood then rush over to give Greg a hug.

"I'm so glad you're back brother. Why did you wait two days before seeing us?" Gracey asked.

Greg was so disgusted by Gracey's nonchalant attitude he snatched her hands from around his neck and pushed her away.

"What the hell is wrong with you. You act like everything is normal when I just lost my wife because of your irresponsible actions. Greg yelled at his sister.

"Stop being so melodramatic, Greg. You know that stupid woman isn't going to walk away from a catch like you." Gracey responded.

"I beg to differ. She's stayed at her brother and sister-in-law's house then told me Logan will be over in a few days to get her belongings."

"That is just for show…" Gracey didn't get a chance to finish what she was about to say because her dad cut her off.

"Gracey sit down and shut your mouth." Greg Sr yelled.

Gracey was shocked. She had never seen her dad so mad. She sat down and pouted then said, "I was just trying to welcome Greggie home." Gracey reverted to the name she called Greg when they were growing up.

"Some welcome home. My wife had to find out what we did from the worse person in the world, Logan. He has never wanted me with his sister."

"I still don't see the big deal. The twins are home, and the rest of the family weren't hurt. They need to just chill." Gracey said rolling her eyes at Greg.

"This family put themselves in jeopardy to protect you now you have the nerve to act like what we did wasn't a big deal." Greg said through his lips that were barely moving.

"I told you guys a long time ago she was a nut case, but you all didn't listen." Glenn said.

"Little boy shut up and stay out of grown folks' business." Gracey yelled.

"We're listening now, Glenn." Gloria spoke up for the first time.

"So, you all just going to turn on me?" Gracey asked.

"No, we're going to get you help before you end up killing yourself on innocent bystanders." Greg Sr said.

"Uncle Grant. I know you don't feel the same as the rest of my so-called family?"

Shaking his head Grant answered, "Gracey what we all did was wrong, especially you and I. Greg I'm so sorry I didn't give you the support you needed in your relationship with London."

"You are so weak. Don't expect me to apologize because I didn't do anything wrong." Gracey said with tears rolling down her face.

Unbreakable: Gracey's Redemption

"You don't ever do anything wrong do you, Gracey?" Greg asked.

Everyone in the room was quiet. "Son, I know it's a little too late, but we are taking Gracey to rehab first thing tomorrow morning." Greg Sr said.

Gracey stood and yelled at everyone in the room, "I'm not going anywhere. I don't have a problem. I just felled asleep at the wheel because I was exhausted."

"It's rehab or jail. Your choice, Gracey." Gloria said.

"I hate this family." Gracey said before storming out the room.

Gracey came back to the present when she heard her name being called then knew it was time for her to go in to get her head shrunk.

On the other side of town London sat in her daughter's nursey watching her sleep. She had only been in this world for three months, but London's heart was so full of love for her baby girl. She tried to forget that Rennie was born on the same day that her crazy Aunt Gracey was released from rehab. Thinking about the huge part Gracey played in destroying her life still made London see red. Even with all the support she has from her family, she was still a little scared about raising Rennie alone. Greg was great with their daughter and continued to try to get back into London's good graces.

London thought about the day she went into the hospital to have Rennie. There wasn't too much excitement until her sister-in-law, Naomi called Greg to let him know London was in labor. None of the family wanted Greg anywhere near London or the baby, but Naomi knew that London wanted Greg to be a part of his daughter's life. This was the first and only time London knew that Logan and Naomi were on totally opposite sides. Logan still wanted to beat Greg down for all the heartache he caused his twin sister, but Naomi was more focused on what would make London happy. She knew that London was still in love with her ex-husband, but the pain was still too fresh for her to deal with him.

When Greg arrived at the hospital it was very tense. London said it was okay for him to be there, but she didn't want him in the room with her while she gave birth. Greg arrived with his dad only because he didn't want the rest of his family there. It would have been good for his brother Glenn to be there, but he wasn't around since he was doing tours of the three universities, he planned on going to in the fall. Greg had only spoken with London twice since their annulment. Both times was when she let him know the progress surrounding her pregnancy.

Gracey had just gotten out of rehab the same day, so Gloria was busy trying to get her settled in. Of course, London didn't know this at the time because she had no intentions on keeping up with Greg's family. Naomi and London's mom Lori were in the delivery room with London. Logan was standing guard at the entrance of labor and delivery to be sure Greg didn't try to sneak his way in there. The delivery was the longest eight hours of London's life. She felt bad because several times she lost her temper with Naomi and her mom when the labor pains became more intense. London was brought back to the present when she hurried to the front door to stop whoever was ringing her bell like crazy before Rennie was awaken. Without looking to see who was on the other end, London just snacked the door open.

Coming face-to-face with the last person she wanted to see on earth, London took a deep breath before she spoke, "What the hell are you doing here, Gracey."

"Good afternoon, London. I know you may not want to see me right now, but I just wanted to make the first move to bridge our families back together." Gracey explained.

"We have nothing to talk about, Gracey. Please leave."

"My therapist tried to tell me that it's too soon to reach out to the people I have hurt, but I'm sick of not being able to make up for my poor decisions in the past."

"I don't want to have anything to do with you, Gracey. You can cross me and my family off your list. We are not going to have you come back into our lives so get that through your thick head."

"Why you have to be so damn mean. I can't change what I did in the past, but I need to prove to everyone that I have changed for the better."

"Tell it to someone that cares." London closed the door in Gracey's face. She wished that Gracey hadn't stopped by. Her head and heart were fighting with each other about giving Greg another chance. She still loved him and wished that they could be a happy family together. Rennie deserved to have two parents who would love and put her needs first. Thinking about it made her sad with lonely tears running down her face. Sometimes she felt she could handle anything, but times like now she needed someone to share her burden.

There were different scenarios that went through her head when she thought about getting back together with Greg. The only person that would give her full support would be Naomi. Her dad may come around, but her mom and Logan would have a fit. She had seen Greg the day she and Rennie left the hospital. She wasn't prepared to see him, but he told her he just wanted to make sure she and the baby were okay. Deciding to take a nap while Rennie was sleeping, London headed to her bedroom.

Chapter Three

Gracey decided to sleep in the next morning after her visit with London. She had a feeling the visit was going to be a little uncomfortable, but she didn't realize how uncaring London would react. Deep down Gracey understood how London felt, but she didn't know how she was going to get better and change her ways if no one was willing to give her a chance. After getting back home she was so disappointed with the meeting she didn't want to eat. She instead went to bed and prayed for another way to make amends. The only contact she has had since getting out was with her parents. The few friends she had was still living her old lifestyle so she couldn't be around them.

Deciding to get up and get ready for her day, Gracey took her shower and headed downstairs to get her something to eat. She couldn't wait for the delicious breakfast she was making to get ready. Having all her favorites should make her morning a little better. Just as she was done fixing her plate the doorbell rang. She wondered who it could possibly be since she knew her parents were out of town for the next few days. Without looking Gracey swung the door open and to her surprise it was Greg.

"Greggie what a great surprise. Come in and have breakfast with me." Gracey said so happy to see her twin brother.

"This is not a social visit, Gracey." Greg said ignoring the sad look that passed across Gracey's face.

Ignoring Greg's mood Gracey said, "It's so good to see you. I missed you."

"Why did you have the nerve to go over to London's yesterday?"

"Wow that was fast. I knew she was not happy to see me but to contact you so fast she must have been really upset."

"Of course, she was upset. This is the first time she called me in months. Here I was thinking maybe she had a change of heart about our relationship but instead I find out you are causing more problems."

"I just wanted to get a fresh start on putting my life back together. I wasn't planning on causing any trouble, Greggie."

"Stop calling me that. What planet are you living on to think that London or her family will forget how you almost killed her twin brother and his family."

"I was sick, Greg. I've been working extremely hard to rebuild my life. Ask mommy and daddy how much progress I've made."

"I'm not dealing with this right now, Gracey. I've been doing my best to get back to my family with London and now you just put another obstacle in my way."

"Greg, you act like you can't stand to be around me."

"Gracey stay away from London and her family. Is that clear?"

"What about you, Greg. Does that mean you don't want to be around me?"

"We have nothing further to talk about." Greg said as he headed for the door.

"How am I supposed to get better if no one is willing to give me a chance?"

"That's for you and your therapist to figure out." Greg left Gracey standing in the middle of her living room floor with tears running down her face.

"Greggie, I need you." Gracey said to the empty room. She was go upset from Greg's visit she didn't feel like eating. Instead she headed upstairs to her room where she crawled onto her bed in a fetal position then cried herself to sleep.

London sat in her den waiting on Naomi and Logan to arrive. The grandmothers were taking care of the twins and Sierra. She tried to tell them she was okay and didn't need them to come over, but Logan wasn't having it. When she told them that she invited Greg over yesterday after Gracey visit Logan hit the roof. She didn't know why she called Greg but knew that she had to get him to keep his crazy sister away from her family. Thinking back to their visit yesterday still made her feel out of sorts. After opening the door and asking Greg to follow her to the den she got their conversation started.

"I know I shouldn't be rude and get straight to the point of why I asked you to come over, but I don't have time to make small talk."

"London, I'm so glad to see you. It has been difficult coming to see Rennie all these months without you being around."

"Greg, I didn't ask you over here to talk about us. I asked you over so you can tell your crazy sister to stay the hell away from me and my family."

"What are you talking about, London."

"Gracey paid me a visit today. I didn't appreciate that at all."

"I'm sorry, London. I haven't seen Gracey since the night before she went into rehab." Greg said.

London was shocked. She didn't think Greg was going to cut his sister off like he said he would. *"I didn't know. I'm sorry I bothered you."*

"It's no bother, London. I was so happy to hear from you. How is Rennie doing?"

"She's great outside of her early teething. The twins didn't start getting their teeth until they were six months."

"London, I wish you would let me help out more with our daughter."

"Thank you for coming over, Greg." London didn't' say anything else to Greg as she walked him to the door.

Now back to the present, she knew she would hear an earful from Logan. At first, she started not to tell them about Gracey's visit, but they have always been her go to since she and Greg split up. She didn't resume her relationship with her best friend, Makayla after the wedding since they had grown so far apart. She didn't want to hear I told you so from her former best friend. She had been so deep in her thoughts she didn't hear Naomi and Logan come into the house. They were told to use their key and not to ring the bell in case Rennie was sleeping.

"Hey, you guys need to watch that before you give me a heart attack." London said with a big smile on her face.

"We didn't want to make too much noise and wake the baby if she was sleeping." Logan said as he gave his sister a light kiss on her cheek.

"Yes, she is sleeping. I should be doing the same since she kept me up half the night teething."

"We're not going to stay long. I tagged along so Logan wouldn't give you a hard time about Greg coming over here yesterday." Naomi said while giving London a hug.

"Thanks, Na. I could use some backup since I'm not in fighting mode." London said calling Naomi but her nick name.

"I am in the room. I not here to fight with you Lon. I just want to know why you would invite that fool in your house."

"Logan stop attacking her before she can explain why she had Greg to come over. Besides, he's been here plenty of times for his visits with Rennie."

"Don't remind me. I don't like the idea of you seeing that fool while he's visiting." Logan said with a frown on his face.

"This is the way it has to be until they can work our better arrangements." Naomi insisted.

"Maybe he shouldn't have visits."

"Hold up, Lo. Just because I'm not with Greg any longer doesn't mean he shouldn't be allowed to see his daughter."

"Isn't it enough you gave her part of his name?"

"No, it's not, Lo. I will not let how I feel about Greg keep him and our daughter from having a relationship."

"Why did you ask him over, Lon?" Logan asked his sister changing the subject.

"Gracey came by to see me yesterday." London answered.

"Oh, hell naw. I thought they were going to keep her on a tight leash." Logan said.

"She said she was still in therapy and didn't want to waste anymore time making up for her past behavior."

"You should have slammed the door in her face, Lon."

"No, she shouldn't have, Logan. I'm not going to never forget what Gracey did to our family and the Scott family, but she has been away for a long time. Maybe she is healing." Naomi said while watching her husband pace the floor.

"Honestly if I had the sense to act sooner, I would have done exactly what Lo said. We can't give her an inch because she would stretch it out to a mile."

"London, we have to be opened minded about this." Naomi said.

"I think we have talked about this enough for right now. Thanks for coming over, but I better try to get a nap in before your niece wakes up screaming for attention."

"We are just a phone call away, Lon. Don't try to deal with this alone." Logan gave his sister a hug at the door.

"Logan is right. Plus, you know your mom and dad would jump at the chance to help you out with Rennie."

"But not Greg." London said with a sad look on her face.

"Let's have dinner on Friday. Just you and me for a little girl talk. To make it more exciting I will invite Colby." Naomi said. Knowing that her sister would make them both want to strangle her.

"It's a date. Sorry, Lo, but it looks like you're going to be on daddy duty."

"That's fine. Sierra will be with Brenda for the weekend so it will give me a chance to bond with the boys." Logan said. Brenda was Sierra's material bio grandmother. Naomi and Logan adopted Sierra when her bio mom died years ago. At one-point Logan thought he was Sierra's bio dad, but that turned out to be false .

"Drive safe. Let me know when you guys get home." London headed upstairs to check on the baby before giving her eyes a rest.

Chapter Four

Gracey was so happy her parents were on the way over to see her. The last two days since Greg's visit left her desponded. She was hoping that once she was face-to-face with Greg, she would be able to show him how much she had changed since getting help. The look on Greg's face was entrenched into her memory. He seemed to only have hate for her. She never would have thought her relationship with her twin brother would be so damaged. Gracey tried to get in to see Dr. Burbank so let him know what happened between she and Greg. He was book solid, so she had to wait to see him the following week. Hearing a car pull into her driveway Gracey came out of daydreaming to answer the door.

"Mommy, Daddy it is so good to see you guys." Gracey said hugging her parents.

"What was so important, Gracey that we had to come over before we went home?" Gloria asked her daughter.

"Have you guys talked to Greggie?" Gracey asked her parents.

"No, we haven't, but we have been out of touch with everyone while we were away." Greg Sr added.

"I need you guys to help me to get Greggie to forgive me." Gracey said.

"Oh Lord. What have you've done now, Gracey? Gloria asked.

"Why do you continue to put me down, Mommy?"

"That's enough ladies. What's going on, Gracey?" Greg Sr asked.

"Well, I finally get a visit from Greggie. I was so happy to see him, but then he started in on me."

"Greg is even tempered. Something must have happened for him to lose his cool." Gloria responded.

Gracey lowered her head and whispered, "He was upset with me because I went to see London."

"Gracey how could you do something like that? You had to have known that wasn't going to go over well," Greg Sr said while shaking his head.

"I had to do something, Daddy. I've been getter better every day. I told Dr. Burbank I needed to get on with my life."

"What did he suggest, Gracey?" Gloria couldn't wait to hear Gracey's answer.

"He said it was too soon, but I didn't agree. I knew if I'm going to get Greggie back in my life I would have to make things right with London."

"Do you hear yourself, Gracey? All of this is still about you. Your destructive behavior has cost this family endless pain." Gloria was too frustrated to let Gracey off easy.

"Getting mad at me, Mommy isn't helping this situation. Daddy, I have learned my lesson. All I want to do is make up for my past mistakes. I've even considered going back to school and getting a job." Gracey was now in tears.

"That is a wise decision, Gracey. We were talking about this while we were away. Your trust fund isn't going to last forever. You need to figure out how to take care of yourself financially." Greg Sr said.

"I just need you guys to support me a little longer emotionally and financially. I plan on looking for work soon."

"You can start with the law firm. I'm sure there is something you can do there even it it's working in the mail room." Greg Sr. suggested.

"Daddy, I can't work in no mailroom. I have almost completed my bachelor's degree." Gracey protested.

"That is irrelevant, Gracey. You haven't worked since your uncle let you work in his law firm and you started so much trouble, he had to let you go."

"That was years ago, Daddy. I have matured since then. I can see if they have any paralegal work I can do."

"Just do something sooner rather than later, Gracey. It's time for you to become a productive adult." Gloria added as she headed for the door and letting her husband know she would be waiting for him in the car.

"Gracey, you have a chance to turn your life around. Don't blow it." Greg Sr said as he gave his daughter a hug before he left Gracey standing in the middle of the floor.

"I will Daddy." Gracey whispered. Feeling like she had the weight of the world on her shoulders. She went to get a book then went out on her back porch to read. She was thinking something had to give because life wasn't going to stand still. If she wanted her family back to normal it was up to her to figure out how to make that happened since she was the one that destroyed it in the first place.

Unbreakable: Gracey's Redemption

Chapter Five

Gracey awaken the morning after her parents' unsuccessful visit to mull over their conversation. She had to accept that even thought she was rude about it her mom was right, she had to find a way to become a productive adult. Her stay in rehab broke her out of most of the bad habits she had before she went in for treatment. Spending money was one of her favorite hobbies. Now she was more conservative because of the many luxuries she took for granted wasn't available to her in rehab. Knowing it was time for her to take control of her life she made some decisions.

Gracey realized visiting London was a poor decision on her part. She was finally ready to move to the next level to make a better life for herself. She decided she wasn't going to feel lonely any longer just because the most important person in her life refuses to talk to her or that she didn't have any friends to keep her occupied. Getting out of bed Gracey took a shower then dressed in record time. There was someone who could help her with her new start. She didn't know why she didn't think of thi s before. Her only excuse could be that she was blinded by wanting everything to be perfect just because she was on the road to recovery. Heading out the door, Gracey had a smile on her face and was able to see light at the end of the tunnel.

Naomi sat at her desk eating a sandwich that Logan forced her to take to work since she never made the time to have a decent lunch. Being back at work was rejuvenating, but she missed being with the twins and Sierra. Since they were still on the small size the Lewis' and the Nichols' refused to put the twins in daycare, so they took turns sitting with the kids while she returned to work full-time, and Logan worked part-time between home and office. She had to smile because through all this Logan learnt how to cook. He was a horrible cook when they got married but now, he could whip us specialty dishes as well as normal meals thanks to the food channels. A smile was on Naomi face until she was interrupted by her assistant saying she has a visitor that didn't have an appointment in the lobby. Putting her sandwich away she stood to greet her visitor. To her shock it was Gracey.

"Gracey this isn't a good idea. You need to leave right now." Naomi said.

"Please, Naomi. Just hear me out. I won't take up too much of your time. I want to first apologize for going to see London, that was an unwise decision."

Nodding her head for her assistant to leave, Naomi continue. "I will give you five minutes, Gracey. Have a seat please." Naomi sat back down in her chair. She decided to hear Gracey out against her better judgment.

"Naomi what I did to you and your family is unforgivable, but I am a different person no w. This is the first time I've been in control of my life since I was a teenager."

"Excuse me if I don't muster up any sympathy for you, Gracey. What you did to my family was bad enough but the thought of you willingly cosigning those two boys to take the wrap for you was unconscionable."

"Naomi the old me would have blamed all of this on my Uncle Grant (God bless his soul), but I know none of these events wouldn't have happened if it wasn't for the family always protecting me no matter what the cost."

"While a small part of me want to congratulate you on what seems like a step in t he right direction, I'm living everyday with the proof that your irresponsible actions nearly cost me my twins."

"I hit rock bottom. I was in denial for so long that I didn't realize the damage I caused so many people. For the longest of time all I wanted was to make things right so I can get my brother back in my life. Now I want to show everyone that I've changed, and I would be worthy of a second chance"

"Gracey, your five minutes is up. The best thing you can do for now is to keep out of trouble and stop trying to make amends for something others feel may never have a solution."

"Thanks for seeing me, Naomi. Please think about one more thing. I want to take charge of my life and become a productive human being my mom said I need to become. If you find it in your heart to set aside your feelings toward me and help me to pay my debt to myself and others, I'll be forever in your debt. I'm looking for work in the legal field and next week I'm checking to see about getting back in school to finish my degree in the fall."

"Goodbye, Gracey." Naomi walked Gracey to the door. When she was back in her seat, she whispered to herself, "What the hell just happened?"

That night against her better judgment again she decided to talk to Logan about her visit with Gracey. Sierra was still with Brenda and the twins for only the second time in their lives were spending the night with their grandparents Lori and Logan Sr. Calling Lori to ask her to take the twins for the night was a big deal, but Lori was happy to do it because the only other time the twins were away from home for the night they spent it with Naomi parents (Corrine and Nelson). Logan was about to leave his office when Naomi gave him the news that the twins were with his parents and she had something important to talk to him about later that evening. When she arrived home, Logan had already taken his shower and changed into his home attire (sweatpants and tee shirt).

"Hi hon." Naomi said as she gave her husband a slight kiss on his lips.

"Let me have it, Na. What did that creep do to my sister now?"

"Hon this isn't about London."

"Okay. That's a good thing because I wasn't going to be so nice this time if that fool step into my sister's space again."

"Stop it with the caveman stuff, Logan."

"How much do the two of you expect me to let go while he continues to disrespect my sister?"

Naomi knew just what to say to get Logan's attention, "Hon, I had a visit from Gracey today."

Logan stared at Naomi like she lost her mind. "What the hell is wrong with these people? Why don't they just leave us alone?"

"That is never going to happened, Logan. London and Greg share a child together and whether you accept it or not London is still very much in love with Greg."

"I don't want to hear this, Na."

"Facts are facts, hon. You and your mom need to stop making London feel like she lost her mind just because she wants Greg and his family to spend time with his daughter."

"Why did that psycho want to see you?"

"She wants a second chance to start her life over."

"I hope you told her to go to hell before throwing her out of your office?"

"Actually, for the first time since knowing Gracey, I felt sorry for her."

"Oh no. You can't let her get to you, Na. She nearly killed our sons."

"I know everything she has done, Logan. After she left, I thought about our conversation. Something has been eating away at her for a long time, hon."

"Oh my God, Na. You can't be thinking about forgiving her for all the pain she has caused so many people."

"Logan, I forgave her a long time ago. I realized her family was a big part of her problems as well as her drug use."

Logan started pacing the floor. "Na, I don't like where this conversation is going. What does she want from you?"

"She wants me to help her put her life back in order. She also hinted at me helping her get a job at the firm."

"This is unbelievable. It's time I take of this once and for all." Logan said as he headed for the stairs.

"Where are you going, Logan?"

"To light a fire under my sister's no-good ex-husband."

"No, Logan. You need to calm down right now."

"She is going to continue terrorizing everyone unless she is put back on her leash."

"She's not a dog, Logan. We need to talk about this like two rational adults."

"No, Na. I'm sick and tired of what's been going on. It's bad enough that she or none of her corrupt family spent anytime in prison for what they've done but now she thinks that she can pop up anytime she wants to harass us. Not going to happen."

"Logan, please let me handle this. You know that confronting Greg isn't going to solve anything. Think about London."

"What do you think I've been thinking about since all of this came to light. She made the right decision to distance herself from that psycho family."

"You may be right about that, but that is for her to decide. She is not completely sure about her feelings for Greg. She is also ruled by fear of raising her daughter alone."

"Na, I asked you more than once to stop catering to her weakness for the fool. The sooner she gets over him the sooner she will be able to find a man that will be a good husband and father for her child."

"Hon let's take the rest of this evening to spend time with each other. You know it will be a long time before we can be alone for an entire evening."

In an instant Logan's attitude changed. No matter how mad he was with this situation spending alone time with his wife meant the world to him.

"We'll table this for now." Logan moved closer to his wife.

"Oh really. You don't want to slay the dragon and be a conquering hero to your sister."

"I will in due time. Now we have pressing things that needs our attention." Logan pulled Naomi into his arms and gave her a kiss she hadn't felt from him since they had gotten back together years ago.

"Now you're talking, Mr. Lewis." Naomi and Logan raced each other up the stairs to have a night of love they hadn't been able to enjoy since the twins were born.

Unbreakable: Gracey's Redemption

Chapter Six

Gracey woke up with a big smile on her face the day after talking to Naomi. She knew she was taking a big risk of being thrown out on her behind, but she felt after her parents' visit it was finally time for her to stand up and be a full functioning adult. The threat of them cutting her off financially made it clear to Gracey that she needed to start depending on herself. She would have so much to tell Dr. Burbank next week when she went in for her appointment. She knew he was going to caution her that she was moving to fast, but this is the first time since leaving rehab she felt that she would be able to take care of herself.

She planned another bold move today. This one was going to be uncomfortable, but she thought it would help her on her path to independence. When she arrived home from her visit with Naomi, she felt better than she had after visiting London. She could tell that Naomi didn't want to see her, but she heard her out. She had no intention on hinting at working at Naomi's firm before she left the house yesterday but after arriving there she felt at peace and like she belonged. No matter what she knew she couldn't go back to work at her uncle's firm because it just wouldn't feel right to be there since he had passed away. Plus, she had alienated so many people there it wouldn't be a healthy environment for someone with her issues.

Gracey had stopped going to church a long time ago when her drinking and drug habits had gotten out of control. She never was a fan of Father Carson. The Catholic priest was too cold for her to warm up to. On the other hand, she had heard so many good things about Pastor Sanders (London's Pastor) that she thought maybe he would be able to help her get back on the right track. She heard that Greg was still going to him for counseling even after his annulment from London. Thinking about Greg gave her the motivation to do what she had to do to be healthy. She wasn't obsessed with her twin brother like she used to be, but she still needed him in her life.

After showering and getting dressed, Gracey had her breakfast and took her meds. She didn't like to have to depend on meds to get through the day but for right now that is the way it had to be. As usual every morning before leaving Gracey called Greg to see if he was ready to talk to her. She only been doing this since his visit, but she felt one day he will answer her call. She had to think that at least he still cared about her since he didn't block her from calling. Heading out to keep her appointment, Gracey looked forward to the day that she wouldn't have to use an assumed name to get in to people she knew didn't want to see her.

Pastor Samuel Sanders sat at his desk waiting on his next appointment. He usually didn't see anyone that he wasn't familiar with, but his assistant said when she made the appointment with the lady on the phone, she sounded like she could use help right away. He had his hands full ministering to London and Greg. There situation had him doing a lot of soul searching. On the one hand he knew why London felt she had to annul her marriage to Greg, but on the other hand he knew how much the young woman still loved her ex-husband.

Then there was Naomi and Logan. This couple gave him cause for worry. As in her nature, Naomi tried to look at Greg's situation from London's point of view while Logan only could see that Greg hurt his sister deeply and had no forgiveness in his heart. This divided the family further because Corrine (Naomi's mom) sided with Logan while her dad (Nelson) sided with Naomi. London and Logan's parents were also divided with Lori on Logan's side and Logan Sr on London's side. The Pastor knew it was time for him to stop wrestling with his thoughts when his phone buzz letting him know his appointment had arrived. Standing to greet his guest, Pastor Sanders was taken aback when Gracey walked through his door.

"Ms. Gordon, I wasn't expecting you." Pastor Sanders said.

"Pastor Sanders, I'm sorry to push my way in, but I was afraid you wouldn't see me if I gave my real name." Gracey said apologetically.

"This may not be a good idea." Pastor Sanders continued.

"I know this is putting you in a difficult position, but I couldn't go to Father Carson because he isn't open enough to help me deal with my issues. And could you please call me Gracey?"

"Alright, Gracey. I still think this is the wrong place for you to be right now. Maybe you can work through things with your therapist."

"I've been working with him for over three months now. All he keeps telling me is that it is too soon to approach the people I've hurt in the past."

"Some things shouldn't be rushed, Gracey."

"If you could just hear me out. I feel I made a major mistake of approaching London. Now I feel Dr. Burbank was right that it was too soon. But after received a visit from my parents it gave me the courage to reach out to the person, I feel was hurt the most out of my past poor judgement, Naomi."

Pastor Sanders was a little stunned that Gracey had reached out to Naomi. "How did that work out?"

"She didn't want to see me at first. I truly understand, but I think I was able to convince her that all I want to do is move forward with my life and to make up for my past mistakes if that is possible."

"I still feel I'm the wrong person to assist you on your journey to recovery, Gracey."

"I disagree, Pastor Sanders. You're in the perfect position to bring all of us together so the healing can begin."

"I'm not clear of what you are asking of me, Gracey."

"I was hoping that you would arrange a meeting for all of us to get together. To start I thought we could keep it small. If I would be able to meet with Greg, London, Naomi, and Logan and after a while maybe add the parents and even the Scotts."

"The timing is not right for something of that magnitude, Gracey. London and Naomi have their hands full parenting their infants."

"Pastor, we have to start somewhere. I can't do this by myself. I know only Naomi would be somewhat willing to work with me, but the healing won't begin if we don't come to terms with the past and work on making the future a place where we can all get along."

"Gracey all I can promise you is that I will see what I can do. You have to understand that this may not happened."

"Yes, I understand that, but I will keep trying because I want to be able to redeem myself. The only way to do that is face the people I hurt the most."

"My next appointment will be here soon. I will see what I can do then get back to you. Leave your contact information with my secretary."

"Thank you, Pastor Sanders."

"Let's pray." Pastor Sanders said a short prayer before walking Gracey to the door. Once he was back in his chair, he thought about Gracey visit. It would be difficult to bring everyone together, but he had to give it to Gracey for trying to mend things with everyone. This would be something that would take time to put together, but as he thought about everything maybe it was time for all involve to face this head on because going at it on an individual basis wasn't bringing peace. Writing down some notes for his secretary, Pastor Sanders had ideas about how he could pull this off. The Lewis twins would be the most difficult ones to convince to have the meeting but with Naomi's help he should be able to make it happen. His final note was to ask his secretary to reach out to Naomi to see if she had a few minutes tomorrow to discuss this situation.

Unbreakable: Gracey's Redemption

Chapter Seven

Naomi sent Logan home with the twins and Sierra after the Sunday morning service. She was so happy that London volunteered to go with Logan. She knew that Logan could handle the twins alone, but she felt better knowing that London would be there to help. Sierra was also a big help with the twins. Now that she was almost eight, she was a bigger help to the family. Naomi wondered what the Pastor wanted to see her about. The finishing touches were already completed on the upcoming revival.

As Naomi sat in the pastor's office waiting on him to enter, she thought back to her conversation earlier in the week with Gracey. She had mixed feelings about the visit. Her head was telling her not to believe a word that came out of Gracey's mouth, but her heart said that Gracey was being sincere. She wouldn't dare bring this subject up to Logan again. He would be happy if all the Gordons would disappear from their lives forever. She didn't get any further into her thoughts because Pastor Sanders came in greeting her with a big smile.

"Thank you for staying behind, Naomi. Sorry for the delay. I had to take care of a few last-minute parishioners request." Pastor Sanders said.

"No problem, Pastor. I was sitting here thinking about a strange visit I had earlier in the week." Naomi answered.

"How has your week been?"

"Busy. I love my family but since going back to work full-time things have been a little overwhelming."

"Remember to take time out for yourself. If you're not healthy on physical, spiritual and emotional levels it will be difficult to cope with all that you have to accomplish."

"I keep that in the forefront on my mind. I must say that my family issues are becoming a little more difficult to handle. It may be because I feel stuck in the middle of my two families."

"Do you care to explain?"

"Well, London is going through a difficult time. I know she still loves Greg and wishes that they could get back together to raise their daughter. Then there is Logan and Ms. Lori. They make London feel bad about wanting to have her family back together. I'm kind of sitting on the fence because I want to support everyone." Naomi was surprised when tears formed in her eyes.

"That's a lot to deal with on top of work and children."

"Yes, it is. Sometimes I wish I could take a break from everything then I think that is a selfish way of thinking."

"Naomi, you should never feel that way if you need a break. There is nothing wrong with taking time to refresh. This will give you strength."

"I don't know what to do anymore. I had an unexpected visit from Gracey this week."

"Really, how did that come about?"

"She said that she was sorry for her past actions and that she wanted me to help her to make amends."

"How did the visit make you feel?"

"Drained after I went home to talk to Logan about what happened.'

"Why is that?"

"He feels all the Gordons are fake. When I suggested that maybe being in rehab has help Gracey, he didn't want to hear what I had to say."

"Naomi now that you brought the subject up that is the reason why I wanted to speak with you."

"I don't understand, Pastor." Naomi said frowning.

"I received a visit from Gracey also. She appears to be determined to get her life back on track."

"Wow, that's strange that she would come to see you and not Father Carson."

"She may feel that I'm closer to the people involved. We discussed her visits with you and London."

"That wasn't a good move on her part to go over to London's. As for the visit with me, I'm still trying to digest everything. She even hinted at getting work at my firm."

"What is your take on this situation, Naomi?"

"I have forgiven her for almost killing my family, but it is hard to get over what she and her family did to the Scott family."

"Gracey requested me to facilitate a meeting between you, Logan, London, and Greg. How do you feel about that possible meeting?"

"I think it is too soon. None of the other people are willing at this time to give Gracey the benefit of doubt."

"Do you have any suggestions on how to bridge the gap between everyone involve?"

"I wish I could say it would work out if all of us meet without Gracey to start, but London and Logan wouldn't want to meet with Greg."

"Since you, London, and Logan will be here on Wednesday for bible study, how about you guys stay for a little while so we can discuss this matter?"

"I'm willing to do this, Pastor. Just be prepared for an emotional meeting because Logan will fly off the handle and London might be withdrawn because of her conflicting feelings for Greg."

"At the very least this will be a start. So, it wouldn't put any additional pressure on you, I will reach out to Logan and London regarding this meeting."

"That would be a big help, Pastor. I will take time before our meeting to decide what to do about Gracey's visit. I just want peace between my families. Eventually we should bring all the parents including my parents and Colby in the loop. They are struggling with this situation also."

"Naomi, I appreciate your wiliness to assist with the situation. I prayed about this and want all you guys to be reunited. What the Gordons did was damaging, but enough time has passed to try to come up with a solution."

"You're right, Pastor. I better head home. If Logan and London bring up Gracey's visits their emotions will run wild and the children will be stuck in the middle."

"Take care, Naomi. Remember my door is always open if you need to put things in perspective."

"Thank you, Pastor."

"Walk in peace." Pastor Sanders said a prayer before Naomi left his office. Thinking of the uncertain times ahead, Pastor Sanders said a special prayer for the Lewis, Nichols, Gordons, and the Scott families.

Unbreakable: Gracey's Redemption

Chapter Eight

Gracey waited for Dr. Burbank to return to his office to continue their session. They had only been together for about ten minutes when his assistant said they had an emergency. Mondays were always depressing for Gracey. While she waited, she thought back on how busy last week had been. She knew that Dr. Burbank was going to be out of sorts about what she was doing, but she felt if she waited on Dr. Burbank to give her the green light it would take forever to get her life back on track. She was disappointed with her parents' reaction to what she was trying to accomplish. Thinking back on her visit to her parent's house on Saturday brought tears to her eyes. They sat in the kitchen talking after they finished eating breakfast.

"Mommy, Daddy, I've had a busy week trying to get my life back on track. I appreciate your visit because it made me see for the first time in my life, I want to be a better person."

"That's good, Gracey. I'm so proud of you." Greg Sr said.

Since Gloria remained quiet Gracey ask, "What about you, Mommy?"

"That depends on what you have been doing?" Gloria answered.

"Well to start, I've decided to go back to school in the fall to finish my degree. I've also decided to look for work right away."

"That's a good step in the right direction. What else have you been doing. I got the feeling there is more you're not telling us." Gloria said.

"I went to see two people, I thought would be able to help me to move forward in my life." Gracey paused briefly before continuing. "I went to see Naomi and Pastor Sanders."

Gloria stood then started pacing as she talked. "Gracey haven't you learned anything from your disastrous visit with London? And why in the world would you go to Pastor Sanders instead of Father Carson if you needed spiritual guidance?"

"Mommy please calm down. I went to visit Naomi because she is calm and levelheaded. Plus, I hinted to her that I would like to get a job at her firm. My visit with Pastor Sanders was to see if he could arrange a meeting between me, Greggie, London, Naomi, Logan to start."

"You must be still on drugs if you think Naomi would lift a finger to help you after you almost killed her family. Father Carson could have arranged that meeting. Going to London's Pastor was totally inappropriate."

"Sit down, honey so we can talk about this in a peaceful manner. You should be proud that our visit gave Gracey the courage to face her problems head on." Greg Sr stated.,

Returning to her seat Gloria said with a disappointed look on her face, "Gracey you are moving too fast. You need to be following Dr. Burbank's recommendations."

"Mommy, Dr. Burbank is helping to guide me in the right direction, but I'm the one that have to take control of trying to make amends to all the people I've hurt." Gracey explained.

"Gracey how did the visits go?" Greg Sr asked.

"My visit with Naomi started off kind of strained. I know she didn't want to see me but by the time I left I had the feeling that I was able to convince her that I'm willing to put the work into being a better person."

"You have to see, Gracey if you keep going off halfcocked, you're not going to ever get your relationship with Greg on the right track." Gloria said after she calmed down.

"I don't know what else to do, Mommy. I've called Greggie every morning since his visit, but he refuses to answer any of my calls."

"Look at the bright side, Gracey, at least he hasn't blocked you so that's encouraging." Greg Sr said.

Gracey jumped when Dr. Burbank touched, he slightly on her shoulder. "Are you alright, Gracey? You were so deep in thought that you didn't respond to me calling your name."

"I'm sorry, Dr. Burbank. I was thinking about my visit to my parents house over the weekend."

"How did that go?" Dr. Burbank asked.

"It was emotional, but I was able to convince my parents that I need to take charge of my life."

"How do you plan to do that, Gracey?"

"By following through on my promise to my parents to go back to school to finish my degree and get a job."

"That is a good start, Gracey. But remember don't take on too much at one time." Dr. Burbank warned.

"They didn't like my other news. I told them about my visits to Naomi and Pastor Sanders."

"Gracey why would you continue to approach people that we agreed was to soon to talk to? After our phone call about your visit with London, I though we agreed to use caution moving forward."

"Dr. Burbank, I agree with you that my visit to London was not a good move, but my other two visits were needed to regain control of my life."

"If you move too fast, Gracey the outcome could be a major setback to all the progress you've made over the past months."

"It's been months, Dr. Burbank. I'm not trying to be pushy. I just want to continue to make progress. Wanting to mend things with the people I've hurt is the best way for me to start moving my life in the right direction."

"That's true, Gracey. You are going to have to mend things with the people you've hurt in the past but forcing yourself on those people could turn out badly."

"Dr. Burbank, I feel positive and stronger after the things I've accomplished last week. I mean no disrespect to your help, but I feel doing the things I've done will speed up my recovery."

"Some things shouldn't be rushed, Gracey. Since you've already made contact maybe it's time for you to take a step back and see what happens from here on."

"I understand. I don't plan on making any more visits. I've planted the seeds, so I will wait for them to grow."

"That's good to hear, Gracey. If you haven't done so, take this time to focus on getting back in school. You only have a few months to get things in order."

"I have been doing research and waiting on an advisor to get back with me to see what I need to do and how long it will take for me to finish my degree. By my calculations I should only have a few semesters to complete."

"That's good, Gracey. For our next visit I want you to work on your short-term and long-term goals. We can discuss how you can go about reaching these goals."

Gracey stood to get ready to leave. "Dr. Burbank thank you for not coming down on me hard for disobeying your plan for my recovery."

Dr. Burbank walked Gracey to the door then said, "Gracey, I'm not here to reprimand you. My goal is to help you to become healthy emotionally. I'll see you next week." After Gracey left Dr. Burbank had to think of a different way to support Gracey. He didn't want to be too confident, but Gracey was making good progress. Facing her battle head on like she was doing would speed up her recovery.

Chapter Nine

Naomi sat in the small conference room at the church with Logan and London. She felt bad that she couldn't let them know what the meeting was about. Their mothers were at Naomi and Logan's house watching all the kids except for Sierra. She was still in the church school playing with a few other kids. The happy looks on Logan and London's faces will soon evaporate when they find out what the meeting was about. Since her meeting with the Pastor after Sunday service, Naomi tried to slyly bring up the topic of Gracey up with both Logan and London but each time they shut her down. So far Naomi had a long week at work. She couldn't believe she spent some of her time looking for work for Gracey. She had decided to help Gracey find work at her firm but wanted to wait until this meeting to let Logan and London know. Coming out her thoughts she wanted to test the waters again.

"Have you guys thought any more about the visit I had from, Gracey."

"Things were going so well, Na. Why did you have to bring that psycho up?" London said.

"Yeah babe, she is a mood killer." Logan agreed.

Before Naomi could answer them, Pastor Sanders walked into the conference room.

"Good evening everyone. I promised not to keep you all too long." Pastor Sanders said to the trio.

"No problem, Pastor. You came in just in time. Na was bringing up a subject we want to forget about." London said.

"Oh really. What subject are you referring to, London?"

With a smile on her face she whispered, "She said the G word."

After he stop laughing Logan said, "That's a good one, Lon."

"Okay. If you guys are done poking fun at me the Pastor needs to tell us why we are here." Naomi said

"London, Logan. I've taken on a task that I will need you guys help with." Pastor Sanders started off easy.

"You know we got your back, Pastor." London said while Logan nodded in agreement.

"I'm glad to hear that, London. I had a visitor last week that reached out for my help and I'm going to need all of you guys to pitch in to help."

Naomi didn't look the twins in their faces because she knew both were going to hit the roof.

"Sure. What do you need help with Pastor?" Logan asked.

"The visitor that came by last week was Gracey Gordon. She asked that I help her to bridge the gap between the families. So, I wanted to try some counseling between you guys."

"I'm sorry Pastor. That's not going to happen. That crazy family is toxic." Logan said as he slid back into his seat with an angry look on his face.

"I agree with, Lo. I don't want to conversate with that woman." London added.

"Guys it's time for us to start healing. We've been blessed. We have beautiful children, a strong support system on both sides of our families, and the Scott family is doing well."

"Baby how can you support this craziness? That woman almost killed our family."

"Hon, I've been thinking about her visit to me a lot. I think she is sincere about trying to turn her life around."

"I concur with Naomi. Gracey seems ready, willing, and able to make amends for her past mistakes."

"Come on Pastor. She can't be cured in that short amount of time." London said.

"No, she isn't completely cured, but she is heading in the right direction. This isn't just about her wanting her brother back in her life but to make a self-sufficient life for herself." Pastor Sanders explained.

"Pastor, I must say I'm disappointed. I feel like Lon and I were ambushed." Logan said as he began to pace the floor.

"Na please tell me you didn't know what the Pastor wanted to talk to us about."

"London, I…"

"That isn't the issue, London. It's high time you all decide how to work all of this out. London how do you feel about Greg reentering your life?" Pastor Sanders asked.

Looking at Logan, London was hesitant to answered. "I want Greg to have a good relationship with our daughter."

"That's not answering the question, London. Do you think you and Greg may reunite one day?"

"No."

"Why not, London?"

"Because there is too much friction between our families."

"What if that wasn't the case? Pastor Sanders continued.

"With time I guess we might be able to give it a try."

"Lon are you crazy? How can you even consider getting back with that man?" Logan asked angerly.

"Hon leave her alone. There is nothing wrong with London wanting to get back with Greg."

"Have you been asleep all this time, Babe? That man is poison to her and not a good role model for Rennie."

"That is for London to decide. Not you or anyone else for that matter."

"Stop it you guys. Now you see why we will never work things out. Na and Logan never argue or disagree unless it is about the Gordons." London said passionately.

"Okay. Emotions are high right now. Let's table this discussion for now. But it will be a good idea to think about what we just talked about" Pastor Sanders said.

"I have one more thing to discuss. I've decided to help Gracey find employment at the firm." Naomi said.

Logan looked at his wife then without barely parting his lips he said, "That will be the worst decision you ever made in your life." After that Logan stormed out the room.

"I agree with Lo, Na." Then London left the room.

"I guess I'm going to have to find a way home." Naomi said with tears in her eyes.

"Let's go. I'll take you home." Pastor Sanders and Naomi left the conference room with defeated looks on their faces. Pastor Sanders thought this is only the beginning of the nightmare these young people will have to endure.

Unbreakable: Gracey's Redemption

Chapter Ten

Gracey woke up Friday morning anxious. She couldn't believe it when she received a call for Naomi asking her to stop by her office this morning. She didn't know what Naomi wanted to meet with her about, but she hoped it was to help her mend their family and/or possible employment with her firm. Gracey mostly stayed around the house during the week after her appointment with Dr. Burbank on Monday. She could tell that he wasn't happy that she was taking control of her life, but she felt it was time. Not hearing from Greg still bothered Gracey. She wondered if he would ever talk to her again.

Today Gracey decided would be the first day since his visit that she wouldn't call Greg. She was also excited because next Monday after her appointment with Dr. Burbank she had a meeting with an advisor to see what she needed to do to get enrolled for fall classes. She was proud of herself because even with the stress she has been under, she didn't even think about drinking or drugs. Before she went into rehab, she thought she would never be able to kick her bad habits. She still had demons she needed to work through but feeling stronger will give her the strength to stay on the right track.

Heading downstairs to fix a light breakfast of toast and juice, Gracey killed a little more time until it was time for her to meet with Naomi. She was happy to hear from her dad a few days ago, but she hadn't heard from her mom since their meeting over the weekend. Gracey felt once she proved to everyone, she was turning over a new leaf her mom would be a little kinder to her. Between her mom and Greg, Gracey was sad that their relationship was so strained. Her younger brother Glenn will be home for the summer this weekend, so she won't be visiting her parents' house too often. Glenn always got on her nerve so with all that she had to accomplish she didn't want to have to deal with her bratty little brother.

As she was headed out the door for her appointment with Naomi, Gracey cell phone rang. She was surprised that it was Greg. She quickly headed back to her den and sat down to talk to her brother.

"Hi, Greggie. It's good to hear from you."

"I was calling to see if you have any free time this weekend." Greg said.

"Sure, I do."

"Can we meet at your condo around ten o'clock on Saturday morning?"

Sure, Greggie. I can't want to see you."

"Please don't call me that, Gracey."

"Alright, Greg. I will see you Saturday morning."

"Thanks, Gracey."

"Love you, Greg." Gracey said but Greg had already disconnected their call. Figuring she could worry about that at another time, Gracey headed out the door so she wouldn't be late for her appointment with Naomi.

Naomi sat at her desk waiting on Gracey to arrive for their appointment. She couldn't believe things were getting so out of control with Logan. For the first time since they've been married (outside of her having the twins) they were separated for the last two nights. Logan dropped Sierra off at home on the night they met with Pastor Sanders, but he told their moms Naomi would be home soon then left. He hasn't been home since. Even though it had only been two nights she was concerned. Especially since he didn't go over to London's which is where she thought he would hide out.

It was very discerning to Naomi to find out that Logan had been staying with his best friend, Simon Crosby who happened to be a junior attorney at her firm. When Simon told her yesterday morning that Logan crashed at his place, Naomi was pissed. The least he could have done was stayed with a family member. She didn't like her personal business floating around the office. Gracious as ever she thanked Simon for letting her know that Logan was okay. Since today was Friday and they both had the weekend off, Naomi was going to ask Logan to come home so they could work things out. The knock on her door told her it was time to get back to work. Once Gracey was seated in front of her, Naomi started the conservation.

"How are you feeling this morning, Gracey?"

"Pretty good. How about yourself?"

"Good. Thanks for asking. I guess you are wondering why I asked you to come in this morning."

"Yes. I've been anxious because I'm unsure if this is good or bad."

"Gracey, I've been thinking a lot about our visit. I do hope you are sincere in wanting to turn your life around."

"I am, Naomi. I just want the chance to better myself and eventually try to make amends with the people I've hurt."

"If you are interested, I've found a position here at the firm that might interest you."

Gracey was so happy to hear this she didn't know what to say at first. "Seriously. Of course, I'm interested, Naomi."

"We are going to start you off with a three-month probation period. If at the end of the three months you or the firm wish to terminate our agreement we can do so. How does that sound to you?"

"Like the best news I've had since I was sprung from rehab. I promise you won't regret giving me a chance, Naomi."

"Okay. Will you be able to start right after the holiday on July sixth?"

"Sure."

"Alright you will work in our junior law offices. You will be doing paralegal work."

"This is awesome. I'm meeting with an advisor next week to make plans to start school in the fall. This is right on time. I will be settled in at work and be able to schedule my classes around work."

"I'm glad you are making progress, Gracey. Keep up the good work."

"Thanks, Naomi."

"I guess that will be all. You will get a welcome packet via email soon. Fill out your application and other necessary paperwork. You will be reporting to Simon Crosby. Do you have any questions?"

"No not right now. I can't wait to tell my parents. I know my mom didn't expect me to keep my promises, but I'm going to prove her wrong."

"A little advice, Gracey. Do what you need to do for yourself. It is good to want to make other people happy, but your priority should be to keep up with your therapy and take it slow with the other stuff."

"I know, Naomi. That is what my therapist has been trying to tell me. I know I want things to magically be okay, but rehab have taught me the art of patience."

"I'll be in touch if anything comes up that you need to know about your new job before you receive your paperwork. Thanks for coming in and enjoy the rest of your day." Naomi walked Gracey to the door. She prayed that her decision to hire Gracey won't create even more problems between she and Logan. She just wanted her husband to come home.

Chapter Eleven

Gracey didn't sleep that much last night. She was excited about her new job at Naomi's firm but the biggest reason she couldn't sleep a wink was the anticipation of her visit with Greg. She prayed that Greg wanted to make amends with her. She missed her brother so much and couldn't wait to prove to him that she was trying her hardest to become a better person. A million different scenarios went through her mind about what Greg wanted to see her about, but she forced herself to stop trying to guess his reasoning. When she gotten home yesterday from her appointment with Naomi the first call she made was to her dad. She was so excited she could hardly get the words out. She wanted to visit but she didn't want to deal with her mom's negativity and since Glenn was home for the summer, she was going to limit her visits to her parents' house.

Gracey was planning to spend the rest of the weekend after Greg's visit to prepare for her meeting with the advisor on Monday after her appointment with Dr. Burbank. She decided after she obtained her bachelor's degree, she would work straight through to get her Masters. She wished she had stayed in school like Greg. Her parents told her that Greg was going back to school in the fall to get his PhD. As she made her way to her kitchen, she thought about what she should make for them for a snack. She was bypassing breakfast and if Greg were on his regular schedule, he would have already eaten breakfast. Gracey decided to make a tray of bagels with cream cheese, fruit salad, cheese, and crackers. She mad tea for herself and strong coffee for Greg. As soon as she sat the tray on the table the doorbell rang. Seeing Greg on the other side of the door made her nervous and happy at the same time.

"Good morning, Greg. How are you feeling today?" Gracey asked her twin brother.

"Doing well as expected." How are you, Gracey?" Greg answered as he followed Gracey into the kitchen.

"I'm hanging in there. I'm working hard to get my life in order."

"I guess you've been wondering why I wanted to meet with you today?"

"Yes, I have. A million different scenarios been going through my mind until I stopped myself and decided it was best to wait to hear it from you."

"I've been doing a lot of soul searching and after speaking with Mom and Dad, I decided I should give you a chance to explain yourself."

"Mommy encouraged you to meet with me?" Gracey asked shocked.

"Not exactly. She feels that you are going to screw up again. It was mainly Dad that said you were working hard to turn your life around."

"I should have known. Even when I told her I gotten a job and was going back to school in the fall that still isn't enough for her." Gracey said sadly.

"Gracey, you can't blame her for being cautious. Your actions caused a lot of misery and pain in our family. It is good that you are planning on going back to school. Where did you find a job?"

Gracey hesitated to tell Greg that she had gotten a job with Naomi because she felt he would think she was scheming. "I will start work after the holiday at Naomi's firm."

The disbelief on Greg's face confirmed Gracey's suspicion. "I hope you are joking, Gracey."

"No, Greggie. I couldn't go back to Uncle Grant's firm. Since my goal is to try to make up to all the people, I've hurt I thought it would be a good idea to start with, Naomi."

"You can't be in your right mind if you thought that was a good idea. Haven't you caused that family enough pain?"

"How am I supposed to get better if I don't confront the issues that caused me to destroy my life along with several other lives?"

"Harassing London wasn't enough? Now you have to bring her brother's family into your craziness."

"Greg, I'm not trying to harass anyone. I went to see Naomi a while back. She was receptive to my visit. When I told her, I was going back to school and looking for work, she believed I'm trying to better myself."

"Do you realize how much chaos this will create for that family. London and Logan don't want to have anything to do with our family. Naomi is the only one I communicate with to see my daughter."

"Greggie, my working for Naomi isn't going to affect your visits with your daughter."

"Yes, the hell it will. Do you realize this will divide this family? Logan more than London has it out for our family. Your working with his wife will cause trouble in that marriage. And I told you to stop calling me that hideous name."

"If that were the case why would she offer me the job. I don't want to make trouble. I want to make amends."

"Well, you're going about it the wrong way. Why do you continue to rock the boat? Maybe in time that family will learn to accept how you nearly killed their children."

"You don't have to be so mean, Greg. I know the damaged I've caused. I can't change my actions of the past. The only thing I can do now is work hard to make sure I don't go down that road again."

"I think it was a mistake coming here today." Greg stood to leave.

"Wait, Greg. Please sit back down."

Greg hesitated for a few moments before sitting back down. "I don't think there is anything else for us to talk about, Gracey."

"I know you don't believe I'm not out to make trouble. Come with me next week to my therapist appointment. Dr. Burbank can tell you how he has mapped out ways I can stay on the right path."

"According to Mom, you have not been following your therapist advice."

"We don't agree on everything, Greg, but I've made progress with the steps I'm taking too. Dr. Burbank's job in to guide me in the right direction, but I still have to put in the heavy work."

"I don't think I'm ready to get that involved again with you, Gracey. I came over today to open the lines of communication."

"I really appreciate you doing that, Greg. But you would be able to see firsthand the progress I'm making if you come to my appointment with me."

"I have to go, Gracey. I will let you know if I can make it by tomorrow evening. Take care." This time Greg stood then headed for the door.

"I will, Greg. Thank you for taking this big step today. I know it couldn't have been easy for you." Gracey walked Greg to the door then watched him get into his car. She prayed that Greg would go with her to her appointment so he could see that she was telling him the truth. Sometimes she found it hard to get along with her mom. Why would she send even more doubts Greg's way? Greg was close to their mom and usually would take her word over their dad's. Now Gracey knew she would have to work harder to get her mom on her side. This would go a long way on mending her side of the family. Going back to the kitchen then looking at the tray neither of them touched Gracey poured out the coffee and reheated her tea. She put the rest of the food away then headed upstairs once her tea was ready.

Chapter Twelve

While Gracey was having her meeting with Greg on the other side of town Naomi sat in her family room waiting on Logan to arrive. She couldn't believe how nervous she was to have a sit down with her husband. They hadn't talked or seen each other since he left home. They were communicating via text. Naomi demanded this meeting today because she missed her husband, but more importantly the children missed their dad. It was easier explaining Logan's absence to the twins, but Sierra was getting suspicious.

Naomi felt confident after their talk today that Logan would agree to return home. She would have a lot of explaining to do because her decision to hire Gracey at the firm would set Logan off again. Naomi planned this meeting carefully. Sierra was with Brenda. Her mom and Colby came by to pick the twins up an hour ago. Since Logan hadn't seen the children since he left, Naomi knew he would be disappointed that they weren't home. She was hoping they would make up and go pick the twins up together after their talk. While she waited on Logan, she thought about her conversation with London yesterday.

"London, I don't understand why Logan won't come home to work things out." Naomi said close to tears.

"Na, Lo is deeply hurt. He feels like we were ambushed the other night. I need to be honest. I feel the same way too."

"How do you guys think we will get pass what happen if we don't work on trying to bridge the gap between our families?"

"Gracey is bad news, Na."

"London people change. You should realize that more than anyone."

"Come on, Na. I was nowhere near as bad as Gracey. I didn't almost take out an entire family or arrange for two teenagers to cop to a crime they didn't commit."

"But remember your actions caused Logan and I five years of our lives. You couldn't let go of Logan just like Gracey couldn't let go of Greg."

London was quiet for a minute. "Na, she almost killed the twins." London said softly.

"I know better than anyone all the crimes Gracey committed. Just like you've changed there is a possibility that Gracey has changed also." Naomi came back to the present when Logan touched her lightly on her shoulder.

"Logan are you trying to give me a heart attacked. Why didn't you let me know you were here?" Naomi asked.

"I called your name as soon as I walked into the house. I thought you were upstairs or something since you didn't answered."

Naomi stood then hugged her husband. "How are you doing hon?"

"I'm hanging in there. I missed you and the kids. Logan looked around then asked, "Where are the kids?" Logan asked as he hugged Naomi so hard, she thought she was going to break.

"Brenda picked Sierra up last night. My mom and Colby picked the twins up this morning. I though we needed some alone time to talk."

"Naomi it's been so hard being away from home. I don't like it at all."

"Then come back home hon. We can spend the rest of the day together then go pick up the twins this evening." Naomi suggested.

"It's not that simple."

"Logan, we are not going to clear up our issues with you hiding out at Simon's."

"I know babe. I started to come home a few days ago. I got into the car and headed home but all I could think about was how Lon and I were ambushed by you and Pastor Sanders."

"I wish you and London stop saying that word. There was no ambush. We were just trying to come up with a solution to bring the families back together. You are going to have to face the fact that London want to get back with Greg. Even if she doesn't, he is still Rennie's dad. He has a right to raise his daughter."

"I thought about that. You're right that is a decision that Lon and Greg should make together. What I find hard to wrap my head around is your wiliness to help the person that almost killed our sons."

"Logan, Gracey have a disease that has been treated. She is still in therapy. I honestly feel she is sincere in wanting to turn her life around."

"I don't know if we should take a chance like that, Naomi."

"Let's take one step at a time. Will you please come home? It's getting harder to convince Sierra that everything is okay."

"I was hoping you would ask. My things are in the car. It's been hell not being home. I think I have also worn out my welcome at Simon's."

"Hon that's great. What do you want to do before we go get the twins?"

"I'll give you one guess." Logan said with a big smile on his face." He gave Naomi a big kiss and as they were headed upstairs, he looked back when Naomi stop. "What wrong babe? I hope you didn't change your mind that quick."

"No, but I need to tell you one more thing before we go any furthered."

"Okay but hurry up. We've been apart too long."

"Please don't get mad, but I decided I'm going to give Gracey a job at the firm."

Logan looked at Naomi like she lost her mind. "I thought we were going to talk more before doing something that drastic."

"Hon it's been almost a year. We need to address these issues so we can have some peace. I'm tired of being in the middle of London and Greg's visitation arrangement."

"Well, we can work something else out."

"Like what, Logan?"

Not able to give Naomi an answered Logan just started shaking his head. "Maybe it's not a good time for me to come home?"

"Yes, it is, Logan. You need to stop acting like a two-year old having a tantrum. I have enough: pressure on me with working, raising our family, and being the go between for the families."

"You don't have to be a go between for London and Greg. I'm sure she will be able to come up with a different arrangement."

"I'm sure she could if you and your mom weren't putting so much pressure on her to stay away from Greg. She needs to handle that head on without anyone interference."

"I didn't tell her she couldn't get back with the loser and neither did mom."

"Not in words but your actions are loud and clear. We are stronger than this, Logan. You need to stay so we can work this out."

"Seems like you have worked everything out on your own. Letting that woman in your firm is the biggest mistake you can make."

With tears rolling down her face Naomi said, "No Logan. The biggest mistake I've made is thinking I have a husband that wanted our family together no matter what happened." Then she left the room.

Chapter Thirteen

Naomi woke up from her nap and it took her a few seconds to come to terms why she took a nap in the first place. Tears filled her eyes again as she thought back to her conversation with Logan. For the first time since they reunited years ago, she was afraid they had drifted too far apart to patch their marriage up. She knew it would be a risk to give Gracey a second chance, but she didn't realize the impact it would have on her marriage or her relationship with London. The deed had been done so there was no turning back. Even if she rescinded her job offer to Gracey, she knew that Logan would still feel like she betrayed him.

When Logan asked if he could come back home, she was excited to have him back. Spending a few hours alone before they went to pick up the twins was just what they needed. Everything was going well until she felt she had to tell him about hiring Gracey. Now a little part of her wished she had of waited before telling him. Going to the bathroom to refresh, Naomi thought she was hearing things when she heard the twins. She was supposed to pick them up later. Looking at the clock on her nightstand, she was surprised to see that it was after six o'clock. She had told her mom and Colby that she would pick the twins up no later than five o'clock.

Heading downstairs Naomi was surprised to see Logan playing with the twins. She thought he had left once they finished their talk. Looking around the room for her mom and Colby, Naomi wondered where they were. A big smile spread across her face when the oldest twin, Lance saw her then made a beeline towards where she was standing at the bottom of the stairs. With a big smile on his face showing all his eight teeth, Lance began to crawl up her legs once he reached her. Picking him up, Naomi went into the living room where Logan and Leo was still playing on the floor.

"I thought you had left." Naomi said to her husband.

"I did. I went over to your mom's house to pick the twins up."

"How did that go?" Naomi hoped there wasn't a problem because both her mom and Colby were mad at Logan for leaving home.

"They were a little icy towards me. I know they didn't want to say too much in front of the twins."

"Yes, both of them are pissed at you for leaving home."

"I felt we needed a little space."

"That's not the way to work on our problems, Logan."

"I think we should table this until we put the twins to bed."

"You're right. Let's get them something to eat and get them ready for their baths." Naomi and Logan headed to the kitchen. Each of them carrying a twin in their arms.

On the other side of town, Nelson, Corrine, and Colby were deep in discussion. Corrine and Colby felt they shouldn't have let Logan leave with the twins. Corrine wanted to talk to Naomi before Logan left the house with the twins, but Nelson said that wasn't necessary. The women thought Nelson was being unfair to Naomi to not be upset with Logan.

"You two need to cut it out. Logan are those children dad. There was nothing wrong with him picking up his sons." Nelson said.

"He should have been man enough to stay home and work this out with Naomi instead of running off to his friend's house like a child throwing a tantrum." Colby said mad that Logan had the nerve to come over to their house.

"They've hit a rough patch in their marriage. They will work it out. You two make sure you stay out of it." Nelson warned.

"We're not children you can order around, Nel." Corrine said to her husband.

"Stop acting like it. That what's wrong with all families involved. Not having forgiveness in your heart will only make this situation worse." Nelson continued.

"How can it get much worse. That crazy heifer has come between my sister and her husband. The two people she hurt the most along with the Scott boys." Colby said not willing to understand why Naomi wanted to give Gracey another chance.

"That just it. She hurt your sister and her family, but she has found it in her heart to give Gracey a chance to prove herself. If London and Logan weren't so bitter, they will do the same."

"You and Naomi's bleeding heart will get you in trouble one day, Nel. I don't think that family have any remorse about the harm they caused."

"How do you know that, Corrine? You have not spoken to the Gordon's since we found out that Gracey wasn't going to be charged for the hit-in-run." Nelson said.

"Why should I talk to any of them. We almost lost our grandsons because of that wicked Gracey. I just wish they all will go away."

"Well, that's not going to happen, Corrine. Naomi offered Gracey a job and she has accepted." Nelson explained.

"You've got to be kidding. Why would she do something so stupid?" Colby asked.

"Because she wants everyone to get along. She's working hard to try to bridge the gap between all of us. The Nichols, Lewis, and Gordons are going to have to find a way to coexist."

"Now you're on some special stuff, Nel. I can't possible see what would bring all of us together." Corrine said rolling her eyes towards the ceiling.

"If you want our daughter to have peace, you're going to have to change your attitude. This wasn't an easy decision for her to make. She had to forgive London for all the pain she caused her in the past. Look how that turned out."

"We have to deal with London and Lori for that matter, but the Gordons aren't our family. We don't have to coexist with them." Corrine continued.

"They are family through our grandsons. There is no way of getting around that. Naomi is under a lot of pressure. She will need us to step our game up." Nelson was getting tried of trying to get through to his wife and daughter.

"Fine. I won't tell you I told you so when all of this blow up in our faces." Corrine took one last look at her husband and daughter then left the room.

"Can I count on you to give your sister the support she needs, Colby." Nelson asked his daughter.

"I guess, Daddy. I just wish Naomi would leave well enough alone. She needs to understand that she can't fix the world. Some things are meant to be left alone."

"I think she is mainly doing this for London. She knows London wants to get back with Greg."

"Well, she needs to cut her losses there too. She may have changed but all the bad things she did to Naomi in the past is a hard pill for me to swallow."

"Everything will work out for the best. Thank you. That will give Naomi one less thing to worry about." Nelson gave Colby a slight smile then left the room to find his wife.

Unbreakable: Gracey's Redemption

Chapter Fourteen

Gracey got up Sunday morning to do something she hadn't done for years, go to church. All the family still attended church except for Gracey. She had stop going to church once she began to use drugs and drinking on a regular basis. She was tired of trying to hide her habit so getting up at the crack of dawn wasn't her cup of tea. Today would be the first time she would see her younger brother, Glenn. They have never gotten alone because Glenn felt his family should have made Gracey suffer the consequences of her bad behavior. Now at almost twenty, Glenn was better equipped to deal with his dysfunctional family, especially Gracey.

Gracey was surprised to get a call from Naomi last night. The first thought that came to her mind was that Naomi had changed her mind about the job. She almost didn't answer the phone. She wanted the job badly. She knew she could never make up for the hit-in-run and the pain she caused the Lewis and Scott's, but she had to move on with her life. Gracey took two deep breaths before she answered the phone.

"Hello."

"Hi, Gracey. This is Naomi. How are you doing this evening?"

"I'm good. How are you doing?"

"I'm good as well. I know it's short notice, but I was wondering if you had time to meet with me, Logan, and Pastor Sanders tomorrow morning around eleven o'clock?"

"Sure. I'm going to church with my family, but we will be attending the early morning service that usually ends around nine thirty."

"I want to give you a heads up that I invited London, but she said she'll pass. Just wanted you to know in case she changed her mind."

"Thanks, Naomi. I was scared to answer your call because I thought you were calling to rescind your job offer."

"Gracey, I don't know how all of this is going to work out, but I feel we have to start somewhere. Please don't make me regret my decision to help you."

"I won't, Naomi. Have a goodnight."

Coming back to the present, Gracey had to rush to finish getting ready for church. She didn't know what this day may bring, but she was sure that she will face whatever happens head on.

Naomi and Logan sat in the small conference room next to Pastor Sanders office. They wanted a little alone time before their meeting with Gracey. They were able to talk over some of their issues last night after they put the twins to bed. Their time was running out as far as private time since Sierra would be back from visiting her grandmother later that afternoon. She told Logan leaving home was not the answer and that he should not do that again when they have a disagreement. Now sitting next to each other, Naomi looked at her husband and began their conversation.

"Hon, I know it's going to be uncomfortable, but you know that you can't sleep in the spare bedroom tonight since Sierra will be home."

"I know. I just needed time alone to process the talk that we had after we put the twins down."

"I know you don't want to have this meeting today, but you are not going to be able to get over the past if you don't begin with facing Gracey."

"I'll do my best, but it's going to be hard looking at the person who did such a cowardly thing and almost ruin another family besides ours. My heart breaks every time I think about how we could have lost the twins because of her actions."

"I understand. It's still hard for me too, but I want to move on and try to make things better for our families…" Naomi didn't get a chance to said anything else because Pastor Sanders joined them.

"Good morning. Praise the Lord and thank both of you for agreeing to meet. I asked my secretary to wait ten minutes before she bring Gracey back here just in case you wanted to touch on anything before we all met."

"I'm fine, Pastor." Naomi said.

"What about you, Logan?"

"I'm good, Pastor. I just find it difficult to face Gracey today. I haven't seen her since we found out about what her family did to our family and the Scotts."

"About our last meeting. How have you been dealing with that?"

Logan glanced at Naomi before he answered, "Not too well. I left home for a little while. I just came back yesterday."

Pastor Sanders had a surprised look on his face but couldn't addressed what Logan told him because his secretary knocked then showed Gracey into the room. Pastor Sanders stood to greet Gracey who he showed to the chair next to him, so they were seated directly across from Naomi and Logan.

"Hey, Gracey. Glad you were able to meet with us on such short notice. How have your day gone so far?" Pastor Sanders asked.

"It's been a little trying. I went to church for the first time in years with my family. I felt like an outsider."

"Sorry to hear that, Gracey. Not to rush, but I know you guys want to get on with the rest of your day. Naomi would you like to get us started?"

"Sure, Pastor. Gracey, I would like to start off by saying this entire situation is difficult. I know in my heart to grow you must sometimes tackle things that may be painful. I didn't think I would come to this place, but after your first visit to me, I honestly believe you want to make your life better."

"Thank you, Naomi. I do want to make my life better. I know I have a long way to go, but I'm willing to put in the hard work. When I first got out of rehab, I thought it wasn't necessary for me to continue therapy, but I was wrong. Dr. Burbank has shown me how to widen my horizon and to see things from other people perspectives."

"Logan, would you like to say what's on your mind?" Pastor Sanders asked.

"I promised Naomi to work on forgiveness, but I'm still having a problem with letting go all the damage Gracey has caused so many people."

"Logan, I know you don't want to believe me. I had a meeting with Greg yesterday and he feels the same as you, but I planned to work hard to prove to everyone that I can change for the better."

"I don't think that is possible."

Everyone turned to the door to look at the person that made that statement. London entered the room then took a seat on the other side of Logan.

"Hi, London." Gracey said.

London didn't speak to Gracey, she just nodded. "Hi. I decided it's time to face the past. Na it hit me hard when you compared me to Gracey the other day."

"London, I didn't compare you to Gracey. The point I was trying to make is that you changed for the better so why do everyone feel that it is impossible for Gracey to do the same." Naomi responded.

"I'm glad you came to the meeting, London." Pastor Sanders said.

"Na is right. We need to find a way to get along with each other." London said.

"I want to prove myself to everyone. I'm waiting to hear from Greg. I invited him to come to my therapy session tomorrow so he could talk to Dr. Burbank about my progress."

"That's great, Gracey. The more you express yourself you will see that it will become easier to cope and achieve your goals." Pastor Sanders said.

"Where do you expect us to go from here, Pastor." Logan asked.

"That is up to all of you. Today is the first step to getting the healing started. I won't say it will be easy, but it will be rewarding if you guys are willing to put in the hard work."

"I have to leave. I promised my parents to meet them for lunch. Thank you all for meeting with me." Gracey stood and left the room.

The relief on Logan and London's faces when Gracey left was clear to see. "I want to say I'm proud of all you guys. You have taken the most important step to closing the gap between your families." Pastor Sanders said.

"We have to leave too Pastor. Out parents' is waiting at our house with the children." Naomi said.

"Of course. If you all are comfortable with meeting regarding this situation, we can do it on Wednesdays after bible study or Saturday mornings at nine o'clock. We can start with just the four of you and maybe Greg it that sounds good to you all."

"I think Saturdays would be better for us." Naomi said and London nodded.

"Good. I make the arrangements." Pastor said a quick prayer before the trio left the conference room.

Chapter Fifteen

Gracey waiting in the lobby at Dr. Burbank office for Greg to arrive. She was so happy that Greg agreed to attend her therapy session. She was also glad that she let Dr. Burbank know that Greg may attend her session after she met with Greg on Saturday. She was thirty minutes early for her session and hoped that Greg would be a little early too so they could talk about her meeting with the Lewis family.

Gracey was nervous when London show up. She though the meeting would get ugly, but instead everyone seemed calm. She could still tell that Logan and London didn't trust her, but at least they didn't get loud. She wondered if Naomi agreeing to help her put a strain on her relationship with the Lewis twins. She didn't want that to happen. Gracey jumped when Greg touched her slight on her shoulder.

"Good morning, Greg. You nearly scared me to death.: Gracey said.

Sorry about that. I did try to get your attention by calling your name. I guess you were deep in thought." Greg replied.

"I'm glad you're a little early, Greg. I wanted to talk to you about my meeting with the Lewis' and Pastor Sanders…"

Before Gracey could get the rest of her statement out Greg exploded, "I thought I told you to stay away from that family, Gracey."

"Calm down, Greg. Naomi contacted me after you left on Saturday to see if we could meet on Sunday morning after church service."

Greg seemed to accept Gracey's explanation then asked, "Was London at the meeting?"

"Yes, she came in towards the middle of our meeting."

"How is she doing?"

"She looked good. It was nice to see that she didn't have that angry look on her face like when the last time we met."

"What did you all talk about?"

"Forgiveness."

"Wow, I bet that was interesting."

"It was. I'm blessed that Naomi is giving me a second chance. I hope one day all our families are able to get alone." Gracey was interrupted when Dr. Burbank's assistant told her he was ready for her appointment. Once Gracey and Greg was sitting in front of Dr. Burbank, the conversation was started after the introductions.

"It's good to meet you, Mr. Gordon. It's important to Gracey's recovery to have as much support as possible."

"Pleasure to meet you also, Dr. Burbank. Please call me Greg."

"Okay, Greg. What made you decide to attend Gracey's session today?" Dr. Burbank asked.

"Well, after meeting with my parents, I decided it was time to start the healing process." Greg responded.

"That's great. Gracey has made good progress over the last few months."

"I'm glad to hear that Dr. Burbank. What can the family do to ensure there are no setbacks?" Greg asked.

"Gracey is on a mission to prove to all the people she hurt in the past that she is a better person. The family can help by acknowledging her hard work and by not putting obstacles in her way. Dr. Burbank answered.

"Thanks, Dr. Burbank. I was going to ask you about something on the same line." Gracey said. Finally feeling like she and Dr. Burbank were on the same page.

"I will be honest with you, Dr. Burbank. My dad is the only family member that genuinely believes Gracey has changed." Greg said.

"That will have to change, Greg. Although Gracey has made good progress she still not out of the woods. The more support she receives, especially from her family she will be better able to cope when things get tough."

"This was enlightening, Dr. Burbank. We will do our best to help Gracey out with her recovery." Greg promised.

"Look at the time. I need to get going. I'm meeting with my advisor in thirty minutes."

"You're going back to school, Gracey?" Greg asked.

"Yes, I am. I promised Mommy and Daddy that I will get a job and go back to school. I want the kind of life I should have had a long time ago if I didn't get caught up with doing drugs and drinking."

"That's interesting. I'm going back in the fall for my PhD." Greg said.

The twins looked at each other like they used to when they were growing up. "Dr. Burbank thank you for allowing Greg to come to my appointment with me. It has help tremendously."

"Not a problem at all. You run along to your appointment. I look forward to hearing the results next week when we meet."

"Sure thing." Gracey said as she and Greg left the office, she wondered if her streak of good luck would continue.

Chapter Sixteen

Gracey sat at her kitchen table two days after her appointment with Dr. Burbank and Greg anxiously awaiting a visit from her brothers. She couldn't believe Greg was going to help her out like he promised Dr. Burnbank. When he called her last night to see if it was okay for, he and Glenn to drop by after work she canceled her nail appointment that she had been waiting over a week to get in. She wondered what Greg used as a bribe to get Glenn to come over. She hadn't had any communication with Glenn since she was committed to rehab over nine months ago.

She hoped her brothers would be happy when she tells them that she only needs to finish up two semesters of school to get her bachelor's degree in criminal justice. She could have gone into many different directions with this degree, but she always had a passion for the law. Hanging with the wrong crowd, drugging, and drinking were her downfall. When the classes and family issues became too much, she found the pressure tolerable until she crashed and burned. Getting support from family and continuing with her therapy would be her go to when things became overwhelming this time around. Hearing the knock at her door made her realize it was time to cut her thoughts short. Seeing Greg and Glenn on the other side when she opened the door with grim looks on their faces made Gracey realize she had a long hill to climb.

"Hi guys. Thanks for coming over. We can have a seat in the den." Gracey closed the door behind her brothers then they all headed towards her den with Gracey leading the way.

"Hello, Gracey. How are you doing this evening?" Greg asked.

"Pretty good. How have you been, Glenn? It's been a long time since we were in touch with each other." Gracey said to her youngest brother.

"I'm good." Glenn said not looking at Gracey.

"You promised you were going to try, Glenn." Greg said.

"I am trying. What more do you want? Maybe I should knell down before the queen." Glenn said sarcastically.

"I know this may be uncomfortable, Glenn. I just want a chance to prove to everyone I'm getting my life together." Gracey said.

"We heard that so many times, Gracey. I don't know how Greg and dad still fall for your lies." Glenn responded.

"I'm not lying, Glenn. I know I screwed up big time in the past. That was because I was drinking, doing drugs, and hanging with the wrong crowd. Staying clean for almost a year has given me the strength to turn my life around."

"Too little too late, Gracey. You single handily destroyed four families."

"I know. With time I want to try my best to make up for all the damage I've caused. I start work after the holidays and I'm going back to school in the fall."

"How did your meeting go with the advisor, Gracey?" Greg asked.

"It went great. I only have to attend for two semesters to get my degree in criminal justice."

"Wow, that's amazing. I didn't know you were that close to getting your degree." Greg said smiling at Gracey for the first time since that awful night before she was committed to rehab.

"Well, since it seems like you are real this time maybe you deserve another chance. We never liked each other much, but I can say I will not make it uncomfortable for you when you come over to the big house." Glenn said.

"Thank you, Glenn. Only time will prove how serious I am about turning my life around. Thank you for giving me another chance."

"The next step is for all of us to get together. How about going over to Mom and Dad's to celebrate the fourth of July this weekend." Greg suggested.

"I think that will be a great idea. It would give me something else positive to tell Dr. Burbank on Monday after I get off work."

"Mom said she will call you so you guys can go shopping one day this week." Greg continued.

With tears rolling down her face Gracey said, "I promised I'm not going to let you guys down.

"We are not the ones you need to make that promise to, Gracey. Greg told me that the Lewis' were working with you too." Glenn said.

"Yes, Naomi has given me a job and is working with her pastor to try to bring peace between all the families."

"Don't blow it, Gracey. Our brother may still have a shot at getting his family back. The last thing he needs is for you to mess things up even worse with London.:

"I won't little brother. London was actually cordial to me when we last met up."

"Okay, Gracey. I think we better get going. I have some to work to clear up and Glenn has a hot date tonight." Greg said.

"Oh really. That's great, Glenn. Is it anyone we know?"

"No, it's a girl I met when I was touring schools for the fall."

"Well, have fun. Thanks again for stopping by." Gracey walked Greg and Glenn to the door then watched as they pulled out of her driveway. For the first time in months, Gracey couldn't wait to be with her family again.

Chapter Seventeen

Gracey sat in the small conference room at Naomi's law firm. She was nervous but happy to be there especially after having a great weekend with her family. She didn't know what to expect when she showed up at her parents' house on the fourth of July. Her mom's best friend was there along with Greg. And a few people from her dad's workplace. She arrived around three o'clock in the afternoon. The backyard was decorated in red, white, and blue. Her parents' and their friends were sitting around the table that was covered with a huge red, white, and blue umbrella. She headed into the house where she found Greg and Glenn in the family room playing a video game. That was out of the ordinary for Greg. He was too stuffy to do something as trivial as playing a video game.

"Why are you guys in here instead of outside enjoying the sun shiny beautiful day?" Gracey asked.

"Who wants to sit around a bunch of old people talking about stuff that happened before we were born?" Glenn responded.

"But all the food is out there. Aren't you guys hungry?"

"We were waiting for you to come and do the honors. You can just bring our plates to the kitchen" Greg said with a smile on his face.

"Where's the maid?" Gracey asked.

"Mommy gave her the day off for the holiday." Glenn answered.

"Come on guys let's go out there and join the others and get something to eat." Gracey said. She nearly jumped out of skin when Naomi touched her slightly on the shoulder and brought her back to the present.

"Wow, I'm sorry I scared you, Gracey." Naomi said in an apologetic voice.

"No, it's me. I've been kind of jumpy lately." Gracey responded.

"I'm glad you came in a little early before your orientation, so we can talk for a bit."

"No problem. I didn't know what to expect. I only had one job my entire life with my uncle. Everyone there thought they had to be extra nice to me."

'I know that feeling well. I interned for my dad's company right after high school. People didn't know how to treat me, so it was an uncomfortable environment for a while."

Naomi and Gracey were now sitting in Naomi's office. "Do you have any questions regarding the paperwork you received?" Naomi asked.

"Tons. I didn't know there would be so many forms to complete."

"Don't worry about that. Your two-day orientation should answer most of your questions. If they don't you can always reach out to Simon or myself."

"There may be a question you can answer for me right now, Naomi. I know jeans are not allowed in the workplace but what is the appropriate dress attire? I have to go shopping, so I want to make sure I buy clothes that follows the dress code"

"Business casual. You will see different forms of dress from comfortable to strictly business depending on the department and what's happening during the day."

"I was thinking about dresses and a few suits. I want to make a total change from the way I dressed in the past."

"That's a great idea because you may have to go to court. On those occasions professional dress attire is required."

"Naomi, I don't want to sound like a broken record, but I can't tell you how much working here means to me."

"Gracey it's time we all move on from the past."

"I think that is happening for my family. Greg and Glenn came by to see me last week and invited me over for the holiday."

"Cool. How did it go?"

"Amazingly well. I thought there would be tense moments, but we got alone fine. Glenn is even trying to have a better relationship with me."

"Now the healing begins. I have been praying that London and Greg find their way back to each other. I know that is what she wants, but she is afraid of the backlash from Logan and their mom."

"I hope they get back together too. They had a great love affair."

"Well, we'll have to talk about that another time…" Naomi didn't get a chance to finish because her assistant came in to let Gracey know it was time for her to go into orientation.

Gracey was at home relaxing after a long day at the office. There was so much information thrown at her she didn't know if she would ever be able to grasp it all. Even though she was tired she felt excited about completing her first full day at work. She only saw Naomi for a hot second before she left the office at five o'clock. From the looks of it, Naomi would be there another hour or so. She was happy she got a chance to meet her supervisor. She couldn't believer how breathtakingly handsome he was. It was hard to believe that he and Logan were best friends. They were totally opposite. Logan was kind of quiet until you got him worked up whereas Simon was extremely outgoing. Their conversation was brief but memorable.

"You must be the Gracey that I've hear so much about?" Simon said.

"Yes, I am, and you are?"

"I'm Simon the lucky fellow that you will be reporting to."

"Oh, sorry about that. How are you doing Mr…"

"We're all on first name basis around here, Gracey."

"Okay. It's good to meet you, Simon."

"The pleasure is all mine. Make sure you stop by my office tomorrow after orientation."

"Sure. Where is your office?" Gracey asked.

"It's on the fourth floor not too far from Naomi's. I will send my assistant down to get you once the orientation has ended. Gotta run now." Simon was out the door before Gracey could say goodbye

Back to the present, Gracey couldn't keep the big smile off her face. She had the feeling she was going to love getting up every morning for work. She hoped she would soon make some new friends. She would love to have people over to share her place with every now and then. Finishing her bath, Gracey went downstairs to make her dinner. Now she wished she had brought some of the tons of food that was left over at her parents' house from the holiday. Soup and salad sound good so set out to make dinner so she could have an early night. She wanted to be refreshed when she met Simon again.

Chapter Eighteen

Gracey had been home for a few hours. She had already eaten her dinner then decided to go over the tons of paperwork she still didn't understand from her new job. After three full days of work, Gracey realized why some people came home from work exhausted. She was so happy that her desk was right outside of Simon's office. They had a lot of contact at work today. It was hard for her to concentrate when he was around. She couldn't wait to talk to Dr. Burbank at her next appointment about her feelings. She didn't know if she was crushing on Simon or what she just knew that she felt the need to be in his present as much as possible.

Never being in love before, Gracey tried to put a name to what she was feeling. Only knowing him for a few days it couldn't be love she was feeling for him. She missed not seeing Naomi at work today. She had the day off. Gracey hoped it wasn't because something was wrong with her or her family. The word around the office Naomi never take off from work unless it was an emergency. She had just finished taking the dishes out of the dishwasher when her doorbell rang. She couldn't imagine who would be visiting her at this hour of the night even though it was only seven thirty. Looking through her peephole Gracey was surprised to see Colby standing on the other side of the door.

"Hi, Colby. What brings you by this late at night?" Gracey asked.

"I think it's time we had a woman-to-woman talk about my sister." Colby responded.

"Okay, come on in and have a seat." Gracey led Colby to her den.

"Listen, I wrestled with the decision or whether or not I should come talk to you."

"I kind of get the feeling of what you want to talk about. Colby."

"Well let me make it clear why I'm here. I'm worried about Naomi."

"Is something wrong with Naomi?"

"Yes, I think there is. I think she is making a big mistake giving you a second chance."

"Colby, I can see why you are concerned about this, but I'm really working very hard to turn my life around."

"That may be true, but you are causing more pain by involving Naomi is your journey to self-improvement."

"I'm not sure I understand."

"Well let me make it clear to you. She and Logan had almost a perfect marriage until Naomi decided to give you another chance. Not only are they having major disagreements about you, but he even moved out for a little while."

"Oh my God. I had no idea."

"He's back home now, but I'm sure things are still a little tense for them. They have lost so much in their young lives. First, there was London on the mission to keep them apart. Now it's you that is driving a wedge between them."

"That most certainly wasn't my intention, Colby. My first visit to Naomi was to just to let her know how sorry I was for the damaged I caused in the past. She was so forgiving and understanding. After a while it was so easy to talk to her. I felt this was the first step to bridging our families back together."

"I'm not going to keep you any longer. I just wanted to warn you that I will be keeping an eye on this situation. If I see that you are just using my sister, it's not going to work out well for you."

"Colby, you don't have to threaten me. I've come to respect Naomi. I don't want to do anything that will hurt her or anyone else in your family."

"I've said my piece. I'm not kind natured like Naomi. I won't have any problem putting you in your place if you dare to hurt my sister again." Colby stood then headed for the door.

"Thank you for coming over, Colby. I promise you all I want is peace between all our families." Gracey watched as Colby got into her car and pulled off. What was she supposed to do now? She had no idea what Naomi was going through just to give her another chance. She will say an extra prayer tonight because she needed strength to stay on the right path.

Naomi, Logan, and London were sitting in the bible study room waiting on Sierra's class to finish up. The adult class ended early since there were only a few people that attended that night. London thought they should have canceled the adult class since they knew that most of the study group would not be attending. Naomi decided against it since they had to be there with Sierra, and she didn't want to let the group down seeing that she was the Bible study group leader. As they sat around the table Naomi decided to check in with London since this was her first week back to work since having Rennie.

"How was your first week back at work, London?" Naomi asked.

"It was hard being away from Rennie. I know I droved Mama and Brooke crazy checking up on the baby so much."

Logan smiled as he remembered how Naomi had the same problem when she went back to work full-time. "That sounds familiar."

"Don't you dare start that mess, Logan. I wasn't the only one checking in on the twins." Naomi said.

"I know. But I do seem to recall you were the only one making surprised visits." Longan replied.

"To get back to you, London. Were there any big changes you had to face."

A sad look spread across London's face. "Yes, a very big one called Troy Tyson."

Naomi and Logan were shocked to hear London's ex-husband's name come up in their conversation. "What are you talking about, Lon?" Logan asked.

"It seems like my dear ex-husband in working in the marketing department."

"Wow. How did it feel seeing him again?" Naomi asked.

"It was painful, but it made me realize the decision I've made is the is right for me and Rennie."

Logan knew what was coming but didn't want to have another disagreement with Naomi. "What decision is that Lon?"

"I've decided to work on my relationship with Greg." London said not looking at her brother.

"That's great news, London." Naomi said.

"I don't see what so great about it, babe." Logan said in a disappointed voice.

"Don't start, Lo. I know you and Mama not going to agree with my decision. I've been thinking about this ever since we met about Gracey. I finally agree with Na. It's time we leave the past behind."

"Of course, in the end it's your decision, Lon. Make sure you take things slow. I don't want you to get hurt again and please don't rush into things just because you ran into that fool Troy."

"I will admit seeing Troy again was disturbing, but I've been wanting this for a while now."

"Let me know if there is anything, we can do to help you, London." Naomi said.

"Thanks, Na. I know I will need support. I haven't reached out to Greg yet, but I was planning on getting in touch with him tomorrow to see if we could meet for dinner Friday night."

"Do you need us to take care of Reenie?"

"Thanks for the offer, Na, but I think it's time we started to act like a family."

"You're right. I hope things work out for the three of you. The few days Logan was gone helped me to see quickly I don't want to be a single parent."

"Babe there was no chance of that. I will always be there for you and our kids." Logan said passionately.

"You better be there for them, Lo. Na is the best thing that ever happened to you." London said.

"I know. Sometimes male pride can lead you down a dark and lonely road."

"Okay. Enough on that subject. Let's talk about…" Naomi didn't get a chance to finish her sentence because Sierra ran into the room full of excitement about the play they were working on. She couldn't stop talking about how well the rehearsal went that night. Packing up their things the Lewis' decided it was time to get home to relieve their parents from the younger children. With a big smile on her face as she closed the study room door, Naomi thought how good it felt to finally start on the healing process their families needed so badly.

Chapter Nineteen

It was Friday morning. Gracey decided to go into work an hour early so she could talk to Naomi before she got her workday started. She didn't know exactly how she should approach Naomi since her talk with Colby, but she knew she had to reach out to her asap. It bothered Gracey that Naomi had to pay big time for helping her out. She needed Naomi's help, but she didn't want to be the cause of coming between the couple. From what she could see and heard Naomi and Logan's love story were one for the record book. The obstacles they had to overcome to be together were not only encouraging but inspiring. Knocking on Naomi's door Gracey prepared herself for a difficult talk.

"Good morning, Naomi. Do you have a few minutes?" Gracey asked.

"Sure. Come on in, Gracey." Naomi said closing the folder on a new brief she was working on.

With tears in her eyes Gracey said. "Naomi, I'm so sorry."

"What's the matter, Gracey?"

"I had a visit from your sister the other night. She told me about the problems I've caused in your marriage."

Naomi was surprised then mad about what Gracey said. "Colby came to see you?"

"Yes. She said that you and Logan were having marital problems because you were helping me. She also warned me that I better be real about wanting to change my life."

"Gracey, I'm sorry that Colby took it upon herself to interfere into something that is none of her business."

"I don't want to get too personal, Naomi, but is it true. Did Logan leave home?"

Feeling uncomfortable talking about her personal life, Naomi wanted to say as little as possible. "Gracey, you don't have to worry about me and Logan. I'm sorry that Colby bothered you. It won't happen again."

Seeing that Naomi didn't want to discuss this matter any further. Gracey decided it was time for her to leave. "I'll go now so you can get your day started, Naomi. Again, I'm sorry if I've caused you any pain." Gracey gave Naomi a brief smile before she left her office.

London sat nervously at her kitchen table waiting on Greg to arrive. Calling Greg last night to invite him over for dinner was the hardest thing she had to do in a long time. She didn't know how this all will work out, but she hoped that one day she and Greg would be able to work pass their issues and raise their daughter together. She still worried about her mom and Logan reactions, but she couldn't let that stop her. Naomi's support meant the world to her. She was the main reason why she was able to get up the nerve to make this decision.

Seeing Tyson when she got back to work was unsettling. She thought he was part of her past she would never have to deal with again. He hurt her badly. Knowing she made a big mistake marrying Tyson didn't sit well. She come to realize making mistakes when you're young gives you the wisdom needed to make informed decisions for the future. In her heart her future was with Greg. She had tried for months to get over her feelings for Greg. Seeing Tyson made her realize she was finally able to make adult decisions with her head not just her heart. Coming out of her thoughts when she heard the doorbell, London went to answer her door.

"Hi, Greg. Hope you've been doing well?" London said.

"Yes, I've been hanging in there. I was surprised and happy to get a call for you last night. Is everything ok?"

"Yes. I just thought it was time for us to have a talk." London said feeling kind of shy around Greg.

"Sure. Something smells good."

"That's our dinner. I thought we could eat before we talk. Rennie should be up from her nap shortly."

"Good. I can't wait to see her again. She gets bigger every time I see her."

London felt bad. That is another reason she wanted to patch things up with Greg. She knew he was a great dad and Rennie needed him in her life. "We'll eat in the kitchen then you can head to the living room while I clean up."

Greg was happy to see most of his favorites set up on the kitchen table. He hoped that this meant London was softening up towards him. "Everything looks great."

"Thanks." London said as she and Greg ate in silence. As soon as they finished eating, they heard Rennie waking up through the monitor. Greg offered to take care of her while London cleaned. Once she was finished, she joined Greg and Rennie in the living room. Greg was rocking Rennie to sleep after feeding her.

"Thank you for inviting me over tonight, London. It means the world to me to be here with you and Rennie."

Feeling uncomfortable again London responded. "Greg, I don't know what the future holds for us, but I do know that I want you to be a bigger part of our daughter's life."

"I hope I'm not being too forward, London, but what about me being a bigger part of your life. I miss you so much."

"Greg, I miss you too. I've been doing a lot of thinking lately. I'm scared of being hurt again, but Naomi gave me the courage to move forward with my life. I know deep down I want us to be a family but taking that first step in scary."

"I understand completely, London. I've been doing a lot of soul searching also. I will do whatever it takes to bring our family back together. I was thinking maybe we could start with counseling with Pastor Sanders."

"I do think we could benefit from counseling. I thought about Pastor Sanders then on the other hand I was thinking maybe we should start fresh with someone new."

"Whatever you want is fine with me."

"Don't take this the wrong way, but I know Father Carson wouldn't be the right person to help us with our issues."

"You're absolutely right. He didn't cross my mind at all." Greg agreed. Laying Rennie down in her baby bed that was set up in the living room, Greg sat next to London on her loveseat.

"I think we better call it a night, Greg." London said moving over a little when Greg got too close.

"Sure."

"We're having a meeting with Pastor Sanders tomorrow morning at ten o'clock. You're welcome to join us if you like."

"I'll be there." Greg said standing while getting ready to leave.

"Greg, I don't want to rush into anything. I hope you understand where I'm coming from?"

"Yes, I do, London. Take care and I'll see you in the morning." Greg wanted to give London a hug but knew it was too soon.

"Thanks for coming over tonight, Greg." London walked Greg to the door then stood there with tears rolling down her face wondering if she would ever feel comfortable being around Greg again.

Chapter Twenty

When Gracey woke up this morning she felt better than she had in forever. She felt energized and ready to meet with the Lewis' and Pastor Sanders this morning especially since she talked to Greg last night, and he was going to be at the meeting too. When she arrived at the church Greg was waiting in the car. He told her that the Lewis's had already went inside but he hadn't seen Pastor Sanders. He told her he decided it would be a good idea if they walked into the building together. Now as they all sat at the table waiting on Pastor Sanders, Gracey wanted to break the ice so she started off the conversation.

"Do you guys think Pastor Sanders is taking his time coming in so we can have a chance to talk?"

"I don't think so, Gracey. Saturday's are usually busy around here." Naomi answered.

"How have you been doing, Logan." Greg asked his former brother-in-law.

"Fine." Logan said barely opening his mouth.

Everyone in the room could tell that Logan wanted to be anyplace else but there. "Greg, I heard you had the magic touch when it comes to quieting down Rennie." Naomi said trying to get everyone mind off of Logan's bad attitude.

"I don't know about that, but I do love rocking my baby girl to sleep." Greg responded.

"London how have you been…" Gracey didn't get a chance to finish because Pastor Sanders walked into the room.

"Praise the Lord. I hope everyone is doing well on this bright and sunny morning." Pastor Sanders said.

Everyone spoked to the pastor. Then it was too quiet, so Naomi decided to try to restart the conversation. "Pastor Sanders, we were just talking about how good Greg is with Rennie."

"How is the visitation coming along?" Pastor Sanders directed this question to London and Greg.

For the first time London spoke up. "Good. We tried something different last night. I don't think it's necessary for Naomi to keep taking time out of her schedule for the visits, so I invited Greg over for dinner last night."

"That good progress. How did that make you feel, Greg?" Pastor Sanders asked.

"Great. Like we are reaching a turning point."

"London what about you? How did if feel to be in the room with Greg and Rennie?" Pastor Sanders continued his questioning.

"Uncomfortable. I thought I was ready to move on from the past, but I found myself counting down until it was time for Greg to leave.

The sadness on Greg's face was noticed by everyone. "Maybe you shouldn't rush things then, Lon." Logan said.

"We have to start somewhere, Lo." London said sadly.

"I think you guys would be fine once you all have more visits under your belt." Pastor Sanders said.

"Do you have any other suggestions, Pastor?" London asked.

"Have you thought about having one-on-one meetings?"

"No, I haven't gotten that far. What do you think, Greg?" London asked her ex-husband.

"I think that would be a great way to restart our friendship."

"Logan, have you thought about what could be done to make meetings with Gracey and Greg less tense?" Pastor Sanders asked.

The look on Logan face said that he didn't appreciate being put on front and center. "That's a difficult question. I'm afraid I don't have an answer right now."

"What would you like to happen from these meetings, Logan?" Pastor Sanders continued to question Logan.

"I want peace and no drama for my family." Logan answered.

"Do you feel addressing the problems between the families may be a solution to what you are seeking?"

"Pastor Sanders, I feel time and understanding will go a long way to repair the damaged I caused to these families." Gracey spoked up because she could see Logan was about to lose his cool.

"I agree with Gracey." Naomi said.

"If we keep meeting up and focus on the future instead of the past, I feel we will heal much sooner." London added.

"These are some good suggestions. How about we build on them by having some one-on-ones?" Pastor Sanders said.

"What's your plan, Pastor?" Naomi asked.

"When we meet up next week we can split into groups of twos. It may be time to open up and let each other know how you're really feeling and what's on your mind."

"It may be too soon to work on something like that, Pastor." Logan said.

"Why do you feel that way, Logan?" Naomi asked her husband.

"We need to leave well enough alone. If we keep pressing on trying to bridge our families together all we are bringing upon ourselves is pain and heartache. When I look at or think about the Gordons, I think about how close we came to losing Leo and Lance. I don't want to spend my time working on something that is going to eventually tear all of us apart."

Everyone in the room looked at Logan. It was finally clear to them that he didn't want to participate in any of these sessions. "Logan can I see you in my office for a few minutes." Pastor Sanders and Logan left the room.

"Logan is never going to forgive me." Gracey said with tears rolling down her eyes.

"I think we have done all we can today. You guys can head out. I'll wait for Logan and Pastor to finish up." Naomi said.

"I would like to get back home to Rennie. Mama needs to run her errands before it gets too late." London said.

"Thank you all for coming in this morning. Logan needs more time to adjust to making all of this work." Naomi said.

"Naomi thank you for arranging all of this for everyone. I want to continue to break down Logan's wall. I know he always had a problem with me dating his sister. I loved London then and I still do. I hope we all can move pass this." Greg said his goodbyes and left the room.

"London do you think we can get past this? My brother loves you and Rennie so much." Gracey asked her former sister-in-law.

London didn't want to directly deal with Gracey, but she knew she didn't have a choice. "It will take time, but we are all adults. We will figure out the best route to take to make things better for everyone."

"I have to go meet with my mom. I hope you guys enjoy the rest of your day." Gracey left the room. As she entered her car, she realized it was going to be tougher than she thought to get forgiveness from everyone she hurt in the past.

Chapter Twenty-One

Gracey was on cloud nine. She had finished her first month of work and she loved it. The feeling of being overwhelmed was a thing of the past. Working with Simon was even more wonderful. Gracey was a little leery because she was beginning to have real feelings for Simon. Some days she felt that he was interested in her too, but she wondered if that was just wishful thinking. She had to be careful because they all were finally at a place where they could stay in the same room with each other. Logan had become a little less combative. She was happy about that because now Naomi seemed to be a little less stressed.

Another good thing that has been happening to all of them is that London and Greg were in a better place. It was too soon for them to say they were getting back together but at least they were in a better place. Gracey loved the way Greg now walked around with a big smile on his face most of the time. Things were even a little better between her and her mom. They were spending more time together. Gracey jumped when her phone buzzed, then Simon asked her to come into his office.

"Hi, you needed something, Simon" Gracey asked her boss.

"Gracey, I think it's time to talk about the elephant in the room."

"Excuse me, Simon."

"I know we haven't known each other very long, but there is no mistaking the chemistry between the two of us."

"Simon, I don't think we should talk about this at the office."

"Why not, Gracey?" Simon asked.

"Okay, the real reason is I don't want to think about anything personal between us because I'm finally making progress with the Lewis'. I don't want to do anything to jeopardize that progress."

"Why would our seeing each other have anything to do with the Lewis'?"

"You're Logan's best friend. If we were to start dating, I'm sure that wouldn't go over well with him."

"Logan doesn't have any to say about who I date."

"I'm sorry, Simon. I don't think this is a good idea."

"Are you in a relationship with someone else? If you don't think I'm being too nosy."

"No, I'm not. I've been too busy trying to make myself whole. What about you. Are you dating anyone?" Gracey asked Simon.

"Not right now. I just had a messy breakup with someone I was dating over a year last month. I finally got her to realize it was over."

"If that is the case then why would you want to start dating again so soon?"

"Because we weren't right for each other in the first place. She was too pushy and a busybody."

"I will be honest with you, Simon. I've been attracted to you for a long time, but you know my situation. I have to be careful with moving too fast."

"I'm not talking about getting married, but just spending time with each other."

"I'll think about it. I need to get back to work now. My boss is a real slavedriver."

Later that day before Gracey went home she stopped by Naomi's office. They had gotten to a place where they were talking almost everyday even when they weren't at work. She had come to appreciate the advice she got from Naomi and talked to her about her family and other personal issues. She was excited about starting school in a few weeks. She thought about her meeting with Simon most of the day. She wanted to see if they could have a relationship but wanted to check in with Naomi to see if she thought it would be a problem with her and Logan. Naomi came into her office and sat across from Gracey.

"Wow, you're here late. I thought you would have left since Simon let his staff go at two o'clock today." Naomi said.

"I had a few things I wanted to clear up before I left for the day. Plus, I wanted to chat with you, but your assistant said you wouldn't have any free time until the end of the day."

"Sure, what's up?"

"I need to ask you something out of the ordinary. I've gotten to know a lot of people around here but working closely with Simon we kind of hit it off."

"Oh no, Gracey. You're into Simon?"

"Kind of, but today I found out he's on the same page. I don't know what to do about it. I don't want to make any waves with you and Logan."

"It's not up to us who Simon decides to date."

"I know. Another issue is that he told me that he had a messy breakup last month with a woman he dated for a year. I don't want to be in a rebound relationship."

"What else did he tell you about his previous relationship?"

"Not much else. I got the feeling that he was kind of haunted by what happened between them."

"News flash. The woman he was in a relationship with was my sister Colby."

Gracey couldn't believe what she just heard. "Oh my God. He didn't tell me that, Naomi."

"I'm sure it didn't help him break free of Colby. She was kind of stalking him for a little while."

"This isn't good at all. I don't think I want to get in the middle of more drama. I've been lucky so far to steer clear of trouble."

"You haven't been lucky, Gracey. You have worked hard to turn your life around. If you want to start something with Simon that is between the two of you. Don't worry about anyone else."

"Thanks for your input, Naomi. As always you give the best advice."

"Now get out of here. I have three little ones and a big one I need get home to take care of."

"I'm sure they will be glad to have you home. Have a great night with your family, Naomi." Gracey left Naomi's office then headed to her appointment with Dr. Burbank. She still hadn't made a decision yet about Simon. Knowing that Colby was the woman he was involved with could be a problem. She still remembered Colby coming to her home weeks ago warning her not to hurt Naomi. She didn't know if she wanted to talk to the good doctor about a possible relationship with Simon. She knew Dr. Burbank was good to tell her to be cautious. Even with all the progress Gracey has made she still didn't feel comfortable telling her therapist when she feel she want to move on to a new goal in her life. Now sitting in front of Dr. Burbank's office, Gracey went in then hoped the next hour would go by fast.

Chapter Twenty-Two

Naomi decided it was time to touch base with Colby again. She wanted to go straight home after her talk with Gracey, but she felt she needed to talk to her sister now that Simon decided to move on with his life. Having a heart-to-heart with Colby wasn't going to be easy. Naomi knew Colby was going to have an attitude. They had a tense conversation a few weeks ago about Colby's visit to Gracey. She didn't like have disagreements with her sister because Colby always found a way to say she should stand up for herself.

Naomi was glad when she arrived at her parents; house Colby was alone. Dealing with her mom and sister at the same time could be draining at times. As she walked into the house, she spotted Colby in the living room. Since it was dimmed in the room Colby either was pouting or having one of her migraines.

"Hey, Colby. Why are you sitting in the dark?"

"Don't act like you are concerned about me, Naomi."

"I am concerned about you, Colby. You have been in a dark place for a while now. What's your problem now?"

"Men what else. I just got off the phone a little bit ago. Simon told me he has started dating someone else."

"You guys split up a while ago, Colby. You had to know that eventually he would start dating again."

"It's barely been a month. He must have already been seeing her while we were still together."

"I don't think so, Colby. He's not that type of guy."

"There you go being naïve again."

"Colby why do you always say that just because you don't agree with me?"

"Because you don't understand men. You need to get Logan off that pedestal you have him on before he breaks your heart into a million pieces again.".

"This isn't about me and Logan. This is about you not letting go of something that's been over for a long time. You do that with all your relationships, but you need to cut that mess out."

"I already have a mama that orders me around. I don't need another one, Naomi. That man was away from home for nearly a week. You mean the though hasn't cross you mind that he was out having angry sex.

"That's it. I'm leaving. I just wanted to show you some support, bur you always need to turn things to the negative. Have a good night, Colby." Naomi didn't wait around for Colby to respond. As he headed home, she changed her mind about talking to Logan about Simon and Gracey. He wasn't going to take that news any better than Colby took the news that Simon had moved on.

Gracey decided before she went to bed that night she would talk to Greg about her day. She was nervous about starting a relationship especially with Simon, but she liked him from the first day she met him. Knowing that he liked her too was a bonus. It was a bomber that he just ended his relationship with Colby, but since she didn't have anything to do with the breakup it wasn't on her. Greg was good at helping her to see things clearly. Now that he was back in her life maybe she won't have to keep seeing Dr. Burbank. Her appointment was canceled today. Finding a relaxing position in her bed she pushed the number one button on her cell phone speed dialing Greg. Before he could say hello Gracey got started.

"Greg. You're not going to believe what happened to me today."

"A hello how you're doing Greg would have been nice, Gracey."

"Sorry. My mind is in a million places right now."

"So, what have you so excited?"

"I was asked out on a date today."

"Wow, I didn't realize you were seeing someone." Greg replied.

"Well, I haven't until this point. I've had a crush on this guy since I met him. Today I found out he feels the same way."

"I hope you going to take it slow, Gracey. You've been doing well these last months. It may be a good idea to discuss this with Dr. Burbank."

"Come on, Greg. Don't spoil this for me."

"I'm not trying to spoil anything. I just want you to be careful."

"I am being careful. That is why I told him I had to think about it."

"That's good. Where did you meet this guy?"

"At work."

Greg was quiet for a few minutes. "Do you think that is wise, Gracey? We all have been getting along. Please don't rock the boat."

"Why do you think this is such a bad idea."

"Because you could be jeopardizing your job if this thing goes south. I don't want to be in the middle of any of your drama, Gracey. I think London and I are close to reconciling."

"That's great, Greg. I'm so happy for both of you."

"I don't want to jink it. I definitely don't want you to give the Lewis' a reason to be mad at our family again."

"I know how important this is to you, Greg. I'm praying that the three of you become a family very soon."

"Gracey is that all you needed to talk about? I have an early morning appointment that I need to still prep for a few more hours tonight."

"That was about it. Oh wait. I did have a short talk with Naomi about this. She told me if I felt I was ready for a relationship to go for it."

"I know the two of you have been close, Gracey, but you still need to remember that she is your superior and walking a thin line trying to bring all of us together. She doesn't need any extra stress."

"We are friends now, Greg. She is the main reason while I feel strong enough to handle any situation that comes my way."

"Just be careful, Gracey. Mixing business and pleasure can blow up in all of our faces."

"I know, Greg. That is why I plan on taking it slow."

"Who is this guy?"

"It's getting late, Greg. We can talk about it more over the weekend."

"Okay. Suit yourself. Goodnight, Gracey."

"Goodnight, Greg." Gracey ended their call. She knew they would have been on the phone a lot longer if she had told Greg about Simon. She wanted to leave well enough alone for right now. Her next goal was to try to get closer to London. Since she and Greg would be getting back together soon, she didn't want nothing to spoil their reunion.

Chapter Twenty-Three

Gracey had a little trouble sleeping last night after her talk with Greg. She wanted to do something to help he and London to get back together. She learned her lesson about not just popping up at London's house. Instead, she decided to give London a call before she left for work. Greg told her that London was an early riser so Gracey took a deep breath then dialed London's number.

"Good morning, London. This is Gracey. I hope I'm not calling at a bad time."

"Hi, Gracey. What can I do for you?"

Gracey didn't like that London sounded like she didn't want to talk to her. "I know it kind of short notice, but I was wondering if you had any free time this evening for a short chat. I could come over after work."

"It is short notice, Gracey. Can this wait until we meet up on Saturday?"

"It can, but I kind of wanted to run something by you. I promise I won't stay long."

London thought for a moment then said, "Okay. You can stop by around seven o'clock."

"Thank you, London. I appreciate you. One more question before I go. Can I see Rennie if she is awake?"

"Yes, but she is usually sleep around that time."

"Okay. Thanks, London." Gracey ended her call with London then headed out to work.

Gracey arrived at work nearly an hour early. She wanted to clear up a few tasks before Simon arrived. These tasks weren't nothing important, but she didn't like not finishing up all her work. When she got to her desk, she was surprised that Simon's door was closed. As she got closer to his door, she could hear slightly raised voices. She recognized Simon's voice but the female voice she couldn't recognized. Not wanting to invade Simon's privacy Gracey grabbed her purse then was about to head down to the cafeteria. She was only able to take a few steps when Simon's door strung open.

"Good morning, Simon. I was just about to go down to the cafeteria. Would you like me to bring you something back?"

"Morning, Gracey. No, I'm good."

"Hi, Colby. Can I get you anything?"?"

"Do it look like I want something from this damn place?"

"Sorry, I'll leave the two of you alone." Gracey said as she headed for the cafeteria but instead made a beeline to Naomi's office. Knocking softly on the door she entered when Naomi said come in.

"Good morning, Naomi. Did you know that Colby is here visiting Simon?" Gracey said.

"No, I didn't. Why is she here?"

"I don't know but neither of them looked happy."

"Good Lord. She told me she has moved past this."

"I told them I was going to the cafeteria to give them some privacy, but it looked like she was headed out."

Naomi closed the brief she was reading then stood. She needed to head down to Simon's office before Colby started trouble. "I'll take care of this, Gracey. Thanks for…" Naomi didn't get a chance to finish because Colby marched into her office.

"Why didn't you tell me that Simon was dating someone here, Naomi."

"Good morning, Colby."

"Don't you good morning me, Naomi. You have no loyalty to your family."

"What are you going on about, Colby?"

"Naomi, I'll catch you later." Gracey said trying to get around Colby to leave.

"This doesn't look like the cafeteria to me." Colby said to Gracey.

"I had to see Naomi for a few minutes." Gracey explained.

"Whatever." Colby moved out of the way so Gracey could leave.

"I don't appreciate you coming in here acting like you own the place, Colby."

"You still didn't answer my question. Why didn't you tell me about Simon?"

"There's nothing to tell. You guys ended your relationship. Move on, Colby."

"You say that like it's so easy. What if someone told you to move on from Logan? He has broken your heart more than once."

"I'm not having this conversation with you, Colby. What difference does it make if Simon is dating someone from here?"

"You could have had the decency to tell me that."

"It's none of my business or yours."

"See. That is what I'm talking about. You go around here helping that nut case that just left out of here, but you can't spare a measly few minutes for your own sister."

"What do you want from me, Colby. I came by to see you and you was so rude I had to leave. We have no control over who Simon is dating. Maybe you should get back out there."

"Do you hear yourself, Naomi. I can't just turn my feelings off with the snap of my fingers. I'm trying to let go of Simon."

"It would help if you focused on something else. Stop worrying about what Simon is doing. I don't know what I can do to help you, but I will if I can."

"I know how you can help. You can tell me who Simon is dating. I know you have to know."

"I have to get back to work, Colby."

"Fine. I knew you wouldn't help me out. I don't know why I even asked for your help."

"Colby please let this go. You're a smart, pretty, and outgoing person. You shouldn't have any trouble finding someone that will make you happy."

"Naomi, I'm going to say this one thing before I leave. I know we don't have much in common but the one thing we do have in common is when we fall in love, we fight hard to make it work."

"Colby the other person has to want it too. You can't love enough for two people in a relationship. Both of you would have to be on the same page." Naomi explained sadly feeling sorry for her big sister.

"I get it, Naomi." Colby said heading for the door.

"I'm glad, Colby. Call me if you need to talk." Naomi sat back in her chair then prayed Colby wouldn't fall apart when she found out about Gracey and Simon.

Unbreakable: Gracey's Redemption

Chapter Twenty-Four

Gracey sat in London's driveway. She kind of wished she had canceled their meeting. It was an emotional day at work trying to avoid Simon. She didn't know how she should feel about Colby's visit. When she returned to her desk, his door was opened, but she didn't go in. She decided she needed to lay low. Finishing up the work from the previous day, she waited on Simon to assign her something else. He did about an hour later then he left work for the rest of the day. She didn't know if he was going to see Colby or what. With their relationship being so new she didn't know if she should have asked him. Getting through the rest of the day heading over to London was going to be another stressful event. Getting out of her car she tapped softly on the door in case Rennie was sleeping. To her surprise her niece was wide awake in her mom's arm when London opened her door.

"On my God, London. She is gorgeous."

"Thank you. Come on into the kitchen."

Gracey followed London into the kitchen then sat in a chair on the other side of Rennie's baby seat that was on the table. "She looks just like you London outside of her nose which is like Greg's."

"Yeah, I get that a lot."

"Can I hold her?" Gracey asked.

London hesitated, but handed her daughter to Gracey. "Sure."

"Wow, she is so precious." Gracey couldn't believe the big smile that was on Rennie's face. That smile was also Greg's. Then she thought that's my smile too.

"Right now, she is but wait until two o'clock in the morning when she doesn't want to go to sleep." London said.

"I see you don't look mad about that at all."

"I'm not. Anytime I can spend with my baby girl is a blessing."

"I promised you I wouldn't stay long. If I'm not too pushy I would like to talk about Greg. Is that okay?"

"What about Greg?" London asked.

"I talked to him last night. He said things are going well for you guys. He loves you so much London. Is there a chance you guys will reconcile?"

"Only time will tell. I do like it when he comes over to help out with Rennie."

"Do you still love him, London?"

"Yes, I do, but we have issues to work out."

"I hope everything works out. I'm continuing my therapy, working, about to start school in a few weeks, and dating."

"Hold on. You have a boyfriend?"

"Yes, it's very early in our relationship, but I felt an attracting from our first meeting."

"Greg didn't tell me that you were dating."

"That's because I just told him last night."

"Gracey, I hope things continue to work out for you. I was hesitated about seeing you tonight, but I'm glad you stopped by."

"Thanks, London. I've never been in a serious relationship, so I hope I don't mess things up. The best part of it is he didn't run for hills when we talked about my past. I guess that's because he already knew part of my story."

"Really. Where did you guys meet?"

"At work."

"Be careful. Office romances can be tricky."

"Tell me about it. His ex-girlfriend stopped by the office this morning."

"Oh no. Was there a scene."

"No, but it was a little stressful. I felt better after talking to Naomi."

"She's a good one to talk to. She put up with so much from my brother, but I'm glad she is there for him and the kids."

"Yes, she is great. She is the main reason I'm working so hard to better myself. I think I needed her forgiveness more than I imagine."

"I'll glad things are working out so well between all of us. I don't want to raise Rennie by myself."

"You don't have to, London. Not only do you have Greg, but you also have your family and my family. Mommy and Daddy is so grateful to finally have a grandchild especially Greg's"

"Gracey, I'm glad we had this talk. I don't mean to rush you off but it's time for me to give this little one her bath and put her down for the night (I hope)."

"It's hard to tear myself away from her. I know it is especially hard for Greg."

"Yes, it is. We are finally getting more conformable around each other."

Handing Rennie to London, Gracey stood, "Thanks for letting me hold my niece." Gracey gave London a big smile as she was walked to the door. When she got in her car the bad day she had seem like a thing of the past.

Chapter Twenty-Five

The Gordons and Lewis' sat in the conference room next to Pastor Sanders' office. They were communicating with each other. It was just Gracey, Greg, Naomi, Logan, and London. They had come a long way from their first meeting when Pastor Sanders had to remove Logan from the room. Logan was still standoffish, but he was polite to the Gordons now. Gracey week went by fast after her visit with Rennie. She thought that she and London had a breakthrough and that meant the world to her. Seeing London and Greg sitting next to each other made her heart happy. Gracey asked a question that stopped everyone in the room from talking.

"How about we all go out to have lunch after we are done here?"

"Today may not be a good time, Gracey. We were going over to London's to plan the twins and Sierra's birthday party." Naomi said.

"Well, if you guys don't mind maybe Greg and I can join you." Gracey said hopefully.

"Gracey, I think it's best we get together another time." Greg said to his twin sister.

Everyone in the room was surprised when London said, "If Na and Lo don't mind it would be alright with me."

Logan looked at his twin sister like she lost her mind but didn't respond. Instead, Naomi asked. "The more the merrier. What you think Logan?"

"Whatever you guys decide. Remember I can't stay long because I'm meeting up with Simon. He said he had to talk to me about something important."

The color drained from Gracey's face. Naomi took one look at her then quickly change the subject then Pastor Sanders walked into the room.

"Praised the Lord. It looks like my work is done here."

Everyone greeted the Pastor then Naomi asked, "What are you talking about Pastor."

"I've been observing you all. The lines of communication is open. Unless there is something you need me to address, I feel these session has served its purpose."

"What about bringing the other family members in?" Gracey asked.

"I feel you all will be able to handle that without a problem. Although, I do suggest that it would be a good idea to have that meeting with both sides of the families present."

"What if we run into issues?" Logan asked.

"My door is always open. Not to put the pressure on, but Naomi has done an excellent job so far so if time willing maybe she could spearhead the first meeting between the families." Pastor Sanders continued.

"If we are done here, I'll be ready for you guys in about an hour." London said.

"Yes, we are done, but I would like to say a closing prayer." After Pastor Sanders was done with the prayer everyone left to get on with the day.

Gracey couldn't wait to leave the church. She waited to everyone left the parking lot then called Simon, but he didn't answer. She texted him too, but that went unanswered too. She didn't want to keep everyone waiting so she headed over to London's. She sat in the car for another ten minutes without hearing back from Simon. When Greg came to knock on her car window nearly scaring her to death, she knew it was time to go in. London had the table in her dining room set for the five of them to eat before for they started the planning. After they finished eating London had an announcement to make now that they all were sitting in her living room.

"Before we get started, I would like to say that I'm glad that we all seem to be getting along together. Over the past weeks Greg and I have been trying to work things out."

"That's great, London." Naomi said.

"Yes, it is. We have decided to get back together." London said a little nervous about how everyone in the room would react.

Naomi and Gracey congratulated London and Greg and gave them a hug. London looked at her brother with sadness in her eyes as he sat there without saying a word.

"Lo, what do you have to say about my news?"

"I hope you know what you are doing, Lon."

"Excuse us for a minute." Naomi grabbed her husband hand then they headed outside. "What is the matter with you. Can't you see that your sister is the happiest she's been in a long time."

"It won't do her any good with me pretending that her decision is a good one."

"You need to get over yourself, Logan. This negative mood you've been in for so long has to stop or you're going to push everyone away."

"Are you threatening me, Naomi?"

"No, I'm just stating a fact. You can't expect to grow if you continue to live in the past."

"I don't need this right now, Naomi. Simon has been tripping over the last few weeks and you're out here trying to be my mama."

"I'm not trying to be your mama. I have my hands full trying to deal with our children."

"Let's go back in. I will congratulate Lon then I'm leaving."

"What about the party?"

"You're so good with arranging everything, I know a little party going to be a piece of cake for you." Logan went back into the house with Naomi following behind.

"Logan, you come back here." Naomi said as Logan's retreated into the condo.

Once they were both inside Logan went to stand in front of his sister, "Lon, I'm happy that you've made this decision for you and Rennie. I wish you the best." Giving London a hug then he walked over to Greg, "Take care my sister. I won't be so nice if you hurt her again." Logan glanced at Naomi then left the room.

"I'm sorry he's being so grouching today." Naomi apologized.

"Naomi could I see you for a minute?" Gracey asked.

"Can you guys stay here until we get back from picking up Rennie?"

"Sure. Tell Ms. Lori and Mr. Logan I said hey." Naomi said watching Greg and London leaving the condo.

"Naomi please try to get in touch with Simon. He's not answering my calls or texts. I think he's going to tell Logan about our relationship."

"No, Gracey. I'm not going to call Simon. If that is what he is planning to do so be it. You guys shouldn't be sneaking around like you're doing something wrong."

"Logan's not going to take this well. Simon knows this so I don't know why he is trying to push the issue." Gracey continued.

"This needs to come out, Gracey. I started to tell Logan a few times but its not my story to tell."

"I think we should wait a while before we make such a big move. This could mess up things between them and between you and Colby."

"Listen, Gracey. I'm tired of babysitting people feelings. Life moves on whether we want it to or not. Logan should face the fact that things and people are not going to always be what he wants them to be."

"I guess you're right. Are you ready to get started on the party?"

"Yes. Let's go to the dining room table. London and Greg should be back shortly."

Chapter Twenty-Six

Logan sat in Simon's den waiting on him to returned from the kitchen with their drinks. He could really used someone to listen to him with a sound mind. He used to feel that way about Naomi, but she seemed to have lost her mind with this 'help Gracey' crusade. He just didn't get it. First, it was Naomi now London has lost her mind too. How could she take that weak man back? On top of that she seemed to have forgiven Gracey for all her past sins too. Sometimes he felt like he was living in another world. At least he had Simon to back him up, although he had to tell him on a few occasions that he didn't want to hear how Gracey was doing a good job at work. Logan came back to the present when Simon walked back into the room.

"Man, this is so messed up. I can't believe Lon is taking that fool back."

"She loves him, Logan." Simon responded.

"I don't want to hear that right now. On top of that she is even letting that foolish sister of his back in her live too."

Simon was quiet for a moment before responding, "Logan, you need to chill man. You can't keep living in the past."

"Don't you start with me about that, Simon. I hear that enough from Na and Lon."

"They are telling you the truth. Everybody makes mistakes. You should know that better than anyone. How would you have felt if Naomi didn't' forgive you for all the pain you caused her early on in your relationship."

"I didn't do a hit-and-run that nearly killed five people nor tried to make innocence teenagers take the blame for my crime." Logan said passionately.

"No, you didn't. but you were responsible for causing a split between you and Naomi that lasted more than five years."

"Why are you bringing that up, man?"

"To show you that you have changed just like Greg and Gracey have made positive changes in their lives."

Logan stood and started pacing the floor. "Everybody seems to be losing their mind around me."

"Calm down, man. You're acting like this is the end of the world."

"I don't want to have to be around them at family gatherings."

"You don't have a choice. Greg is Rennie's father. He's not going anywhere."

"I don't want to talk about this anymore. What was so important that you wanted me to come over right away?"

Simon had second thoughts now about telling Logan about his relationship with Gracey. This would just give him another reason to blowup. "I want you to hear me out without going into one of your tirades."

"I'm listening." Logan said. Sitting back down across from Simon.

"Well, this is about my new relationship."

"Yeah, you dodged a bullet getting away from Colby. She's my sister-in-law and all but she's out there."

"There's a softer side to Colby that she doesn't let many people see. I wish her the best, but we just weren't right for each other."

"If you say so. I see this new relationship agrees with you. I haven't seen you this content since our college years."

"Yes, it does. She's not what I expected at all."

"When am I going to get to meet this mystery lady?"

"That's up to you. We go way back, Logan. I love you like a brother, but sometimes you fly off the handle when things don't go your way."

"Not you too. Na keeps telling me to chill before I stroke out."

"I agree. You wife is a very smart lady."

"She is and I'm lucky to have her. If she could just stop being so goody-goody, we wouldn't have people like the Gordons back in our lives."

"That what makes her so special, Logan. Why would you want to change that about her?"

"We're off topic again. What's up with this new lady in your life."

"I've known of her for years, but I never got the chance to get to know the real person until we started dating."

"I still say it risky to date someone you work with."

"Maybe, but she is worth the risk."

"Wow, she has you whipped already." Logan said with a big smile on his face.

"No, it's just good to have someone in my life that makes me want to settle down and plan a future."

"I'm happy for you, man. You deserve it."

"Thanks, Logan. I hope you mean that because I really think she is the one."

Okay, stop beating around the bush. What is this lucky lady name?"

"It's Gracey, Logan."

Logan looked at Simon without saying a word. Then he said quietly, "I know you didn't say Gracey, man."

"I did, Logan."

"Have you lost your damn mind?" Logan asked then started pacing around the room again.

"I need you to be okay with this, Logan."

"I got to go." Logan left Simon's house as he pulled off, he didn't' know where to head to next. He was so used to fleeting to London and Simon when he had a problem, but they are part of the problem. The only other person he could think of was his dad, but he didn't want to lay all of this at his dad's feet. His mom would be on his side, but she would make it worse by getting in London and Naomi's face.

Why was this happening. All he wanted to do was to be with his family planning the kid's birthday party. He knew he couldn't stay out all night again even if it was over at his parents' house. Naomi lit into him about leaving home a while back. He figured she would be home by now. Then a thought flashed in him mind. Did Naomi know about Simon and Gracey? He sure hoped not. Colby was going to have a fit when she found out. He was getting so tired of the family drama. Couldn't they all just live-in peace.

There was no getting around it. He had to go home to face Naomi. He didn't like disagreeing with her. Their love had overcome so much (mostly his immature behavior from the past). He didn't want to jeopardize their relationship. The time had come for him to do some soul searching. Naomi asked him before Greg and London got married if he had a problem with Greg because he was white. He told her no and at the time he meant it. But not being about to forgive the Gordons was scaring him. It was time that he got some help. If he kept on the path, he was currently on he was going to lose his family and that was something that he would not let happen. Heading home he tried to think of a way to apologize to his wife and hope she forgives him again.

Chapter Twenty-Seven

Gracey sat at her desk on Monday morning thinking about the sadness that happened over the weekend. She and Simon had their first major disagreement after he told her that he told Logan about their relationship. She warned Simon many times that it wasn't the right time to openly date. He told her that telling Logan was the best thing. Logan was his best friend, so he needed to accept the decisions he made with his life. She was glad that she wouldn't have to run into Simon at work because he was in court most of the day and she had to leave early for her three o'clock appointment with Dr. Burbank. She was sad when she thought about her conversation with Simon on Saturday night. She hadn't talk to him at all on Sunday. She thought back to that conversation because they needed to have a face-to-face today.

"Hello, Simon."

"How are you doing tonight sweetie?"

"That depends on your conversation with Logan."

"Well, if you are wondering if I told him about our relationship the answer is yes."

"Oh my God, Simon. I asked you not to do that. It wasn't the right time."

"Gracey, we can't live our lives on someone else time schedule."

"Simon, I've worked hard to turn my life around. Logan still not feeling me right now. What you've done has set us all back."

"Logan is like a brother to me. He needs to have my back like I've always had his."

"How did he take it?"

"Like I broke his heart."

"See that is what I'm talking about. If we had waited for the right time this could have been avoided."

"Logan is going through some things right now. It was never going to be a right time to tell him our news. I know him. He will withdraw for a while then he will accept our relationship."

"I just hope he doesn't withdraw from Naomi. She is the strongest person I know, but if she has more difficult times with Logan, I don't know how it would affect their marriage."

"They love each other. They will get this this bump in the road. They have been through much worse than this and came out on top."

"I hope you're right because this is going to be difficult for all of us. Colby isn't going to take this well. I have a feeling she is going to come down hard on Naomi."

"This is going to work out fine eventually, sweetie. I know all the players involved."

"I'm going to get ready for bed. I'll talk to you soon." Gracey ended their call.

Coming back to the present Gracey felt she was going to need her appointment today and Greg's support to get through what was to come. She wanted to go see Naomi to see how she was doing, but she was in court too for most of the day. No matter what happens, she prayed that her relationship with Naomi will survive the upcoming storm.

Gracey waited in the lobby waiting on her appointment with Dr. Burbank. They had a lot to discuss in today's meeting. With school starting next week and all that happened since her last appointment, she was feeling a little overwhelmed. Fearful that she might suffer a setback she prayed Dr. Burbank could help pull her back to reality. After her appointment she wanted to reach out to Naomi. No matter what happens between her and Simon, her job, our even the progress with her family what she wanted the most is to remain friends with Naomi. She felt like Naomi was the main person to give her strength to keep fighting. Hearing her name being called, Gracey was escorted into Dr. Burbank's office. He was sitting behind his desk finishing up a phone call, so he waved for Gracey to have a seat in the chair in front of his desk. Gracey was so anxious she didn't give him a chance to speak.

"Dr. Burbank, you need to help me. I feel like I'm about to lose everything."

"Slow down, Gracey. Take a deep breath and tell me what is bothering you so much."

"Things seem to be going in the wrong direction. I have been enjoying my life over the last few months but the events that happened over this weekend may destroy all the progress we've made over the last months."

"What happened this weekend, Gracey."

"Well, let me go back a little farther. The week had been stressful. When I got to work on Tuesday morning Simon's ex-girlfriend was in his office with him. They were kind of loud, so I excused myself once they came out of the office and went to see Naomi."

"How did this make you feel seeing her with Simon?"

"Nervous. I had pictured them together in my head tons of times but seeing them in person was different."

"What do you mean you pictured them in your head?"

"I've known her for a while. She is Naomi's sister."

Dr. Burbank was silent for a few moments before he said, "Gracey this is not a good situation for you to deal with right now."

"I know. I tried to fight my feelings for Simon, but when he told me that he felt the same about me, I just had to give it a try. I didn't find out Colby was the woman he broke up with until afterwards."

"Why didn't you tell me that his ex was someone you knew?"

"Because I thought you would try to talk me out of being with Simon. Greg didn't like this idea neither. Going off subject for a minute Greg and London have reconciled."

"Wow, that's great news, Gracey. I know how much it means to you that these two get back together."

"I wished everyone were happy about them getting back together. We all went over to London's condo after we had our last session with Pastor Sanders. That's when London made the announcement. Her twin brother Logan didn't take it well at all."

"From what you have told me the two of them never gotten along."

"No, Logan thinks that Greg will hurt London again."

"Is there anything else we need to discuss?"

"Well, Simon told Logan about our dating. They got into a big argument and so did Simon and I. I tried to tell Simon it wasn't the right time to go public with our relationship, but he wouldn't listen."

"So, what happens now, Gracey?"

"Simon and I need to have a sit down. We talked Saturday night but not since then. He was in court all day today, so I didn't see him at work."

"Do you have a plan to keep things under control?"

"I like Simon and I want our relationship to work out, but what I'm really fearful of is that this will damage my relationship with Naomi especially when her sister finds out."

"Gracey, we talked about this before. Your relationship with Naomi shouldn't be the focus in your life."

"It's not, but she has given me the strength to keep bettering myself."

"You have to find that strength within yourself, Gracey. That is too much pressure to put on one person."

"I've been trying since I became sober to forgive myself for all the harm, I caused to so many people. The thought of Naomi's twin's life being almost destroyed eats away at me every day. I want to see them badly, but I haven't worked up the nerve to ask Naomi if I could see them."

"Why do you feel seeing the children will help you?"

"Because it will make it real. I will be able to look those boys in the eyes and know that I need to fight every day to make sure I don't go to that dark place again."

"Gracey our time is almost up. What I need you to do before our next meeting is to take a deep look inside of you and figure out how Gracey is going to save Gracey. Please don't put that responsibility onto anyone else."

"That is a huge request. Sometimes I'm scared to look inside myself. I don't want to see that damage person I used to be."

"You'll be fine. All the hard work you have done over the last months has made you a stronger person."

"Thank you, Dr. Burbank. I better get going so I can have that talk with Simon." Gracey left her appointment then headed straight home but not before texting Simon telling him to meet her there in an hour.

Chapter Twenty-Eight

The week went by fast for Gracey. Her wish was finally coming true. She finally got up the nerve to ask Naomi if she could visit her twins. This happened on Tuesday morning. She still remembered the surprised look on Naomi face when she made the request. She also told Naomi how her meeting with Simon went the night before. Gracey was unsure if she and Simon could make their relationship work. Their talk didn't resolve things as well as she expected. The bright spot of the week came when Naomi asked her out for lunch. Naomi told Simon they would be taking a longer lunch to go over some important matters. When they arrived at the pub around the corner from the firm Naomi started the conversation.

"I had time to think about your request to see the twins and have talked to Logan. We agreed that if you're free on Friday night you can come have dinner with our family."

Tears rolled down Gracey's face as she said, "Oh, Naomi. This is great news."

"I will be honest with you, Gracey it took me hours to convince Logan to agree to this arrangement. The only way to get him to agree was if we invited London, then she invited Greg."

"That's cool. The more the merrier. Will Rennie be there too?"

"Yes. London told me how good you were with Rennie when you visited her."

"I didn't want to leave her. She is so adorable."

"Yes, she is. Sierra love it whenever she gets the chance to spent time with her little cousin. Now I think we better order and eat before Simon docks your pay."

Gracey sat outside of Naomi's house. She wished Simon could have come with her, but he and Logan were still on the outs. She saw Greg's car in the driveway, so she figured that he, London, and Rennie were already there. Suddenly she was scared to go in. She shouldn't feel afraid since Greg was there, but she didn't know if she would ever feel comfortable around Logan. He was filled with so much hate that he may always see them as outsiders. Getting out of the car, Gracey headed for the front door. Before she could knock Naomi pulled the door open.

"Hi, Naomi."

"Why were you sitting out there so long, Gracey?" Naomi asked.

"I was a little scared of coming in."

"Why, we are family. You need to relax, Gracey."

"I'm trying. It's just that I don't want the family to keep fighting about my past actions."

"One day this will all be behind us. Now come on in and visit with the children before they fall asleep." Naomi led Gracey into her family room where they were playing with the Rennie, the twins, and Sierra.

"Hi, Ms. Gracey. It is so strange to have all these sets of twins in one room. I guess me, Rennie, and Mom are outnumbered."

"No, we're not. You can't be outnumbered when you're around family young lady." Naomi said to her daughter then she turned to Gracey, "Gracey come over here to meet the twins. This is Lance and Logan is holding Leo."

"Wow, they are much bigger than the pictures at London's." Gracey said while holding the nine-month-old Lance in her arms.

"Yeah, somebody is slacking with the family photos." London said glancing at Naomi.

"Why are you blaming me for this. Your brother hasn't tried to get this feat accomplished either. Naomi responded.

"Wow, throw me under the bus, babe." Logan said in a dry tone.

After holding Lance for about fifteen minutes Gracey laid him down in his baby sleeper. Taking a deep breath, she asked, "Naomi how long will it be before we sit down to eat dinner?"

"It'll be close to a half hour. Do you guys want snacks to hold you over?" Naomi answered.

"Nothing for me. I don't want to spoil my appetite for the food I've been smelling since we got here." London said.

"I'm good too." Greg said.

"I asked because I wanted to have a private talk with Logan for a few minutes if that is okay." Gracey said.

Logan looked around at everyone then at Gracey, "Now isn't a good time, Gracey."

"Actually, I think that is a great idea." Naomi said then walked over stood in front of Logan with her arms out so she could take Leo. "You guys could use my study." Naomi continued.

Logan glanced at London to see if she would get him out of this predicament. London turned her head slightly the other way, so Logan had no choice but to go with Gracey. "Alright, let's go." Logan led Gracey towards the study. Once they both were sitting Gracey started the conversation.

"Logan, I don't know you that well, but I do know that if you don't face up to your problems, they will destroy you."

"What problems are you talking about, Gracey? Logan asked.

"The major one that will ruin your life if you don't face it is racial differences."

"What exactly do you mean by that?"

"Logan, my uncle and I had problems with Greg dating outside of our race. We were so outspoken and rude about it we did a lot of damage to our relationship with Greg."

"So, you're saying I prejudice." Logan asked.

"Yes, that's exactly what I'm saying. I thought it when Greg and London were dating, but your inability get past what happened and the way you look at Greg when he's with London is exactly how me and my uncle used to look at Greg's girlfriends that were different from us."

"You don't know what the hell you're talking about. My problem with Greg isn't about race. He hurt my sister badly. My problem with you is that you're causing problems for me and my wife when we already have our plates full."

"Logan since we have to get back out there. I just wanted to point that out, but I'm begging you please don't make Naomi stop our friendship."

"I can't make Naomi do anything she doesn't want to do. I don't want her to be friends with the person that almost killed our family."

"I was sick, Logan. Rehab taught me a lot. I don't care if I have to be in therapy the rest of my life, I don't want to go back to being the person I use to be."

"We need to get back out there. I sure it's time to sit down to dinner."

"Thank you for hearing me out, Logan. Please think about what I said. I hope that you make up with Simon soon too. I really like him, but I don't want to be the cause of your lifelong friendship being destroyed." Gracey blinked tears from her eyes then left the room.

Chapter Twenty-Nine

The morning after the dinner party Naomi and Logan found themselves sitting in Pastor Sanders office. They had a long night after their guests left. Logan was filled with so many emotions he couldn't sleep last night so that meant Naomi didn't get any sleep either. Logan didn't want to believe what Gracey said about him being prejudice was true, but he had to come up with some reason why he didn't want to accept the Gordons as part of their family. He and Naomi talked most of the night, so they both were tired. Against Logan wishes London and Greg spent the night so they could stay with the children. Sierra was supposed to be with Brenda for the weekend, but her grandmother wasn't feeling well. When Pastor Sanders came into the office he prayed with Naomi and Logan then nodded his head for them to begin.

"We had a restless night last night. I had a talk with Gracey before dinner. I was distressed by our conversation." Logan said.

"What was so distressing about your talk with Gracey, Logan?"

"First, I didn't want to talk to her alone. I have trouble getting close to her and Greg."

"Why, Logan?" Pastor Sanders asked.

"I could never figure that out, but Gracey pointed out my problem with her family was because they were white?"

Everyone in the room was quiet then Pastor Sanders asked, "How do you feel about what Gracey said?"

"I thought she was talking out of the side of her head. I know my wife think that woman has turned over a new leaf, but I don't trust anyone in that family."

"Why don't you tell Pastor Sanders what else was bothering you last night, hon." Naomi said softly.

"I didn't mean what I said last night. I was exhausted. That woman is not only causing problems for us, but she also has Simon's head all screwed up."

"I told you last night you need to watch what you say. Me or Simon are not being misled by Gracey. That woman is working hard everyday to turn her life around."

"Well, I'm not in the mood to give her a free pass for almost killing us."

"Logan are you afraid what Gracey said is true?"

Naomi waited on Logan to say something, but he didn't say a word so Naomi said, "Pastor I know what Gracey said is true. I pepped it out while London and Greg were dating, but I left Logan gloss over how he really felt."

"Naomi it wasn't true then and it's not true now." Logan said.

"What are you so afraid of, Logan?" Pastor Sanders asked.

"That I'm going to lose my family. I've already lost my best friend."

"You haven't lost Simon. You just need to chill and accept that people change. Your sister is happy to be back with Greg and I'm happy that I can help Gracey to be a stronger person."

"I think Gracey is fixated on you, babe. She begged me not to make you to cut her out of your life."

"You didn't tell me that, hon."

"I was upset that she was trying to play a mind game on me."

"Why is it so hard to think that Gracey has changed. Look at how far London has come from her earlier life. Remember we lost over five years of our lives together because of her." Naomi asked.

"Well, Lon was out there, but she never almost killed anyone nor tried to ruin the lives of two teenagers."

"We don't know all that London has done in her past but that just it her past." Naomi continued.

"It's not fair for you to compare Lon with that woman, babe."

"It's not fair that you keep holding the past over the Gordons head. I'm leaving. Please be honest with Pastor. I love you, Logan but you need help dealing with this race issue." Naomi said her goodbyes leaving Logan and Pastor Sanders alone.

It was quiet in the room for a few minutes after Naomi left. Logan didn't know what to say to Pastor Sanders. He wanted a one-on-one conversation with the pastor for a long time but didn't know how to bring the subject up. He was terrified about the feelings that was going on deep inside of him. Logan had white friends before that is why he didn't think he had a problem with race. If he was going to ever confront this problem, he knew he had to speak up and ask for Pastor Sanders' help.

"Pastor, I'm scared."

"What are your scared of son?"

"Of the crazy thoughts that goes on in my head sometimes."

"What kind of thoughts, Logan?"

"That London could do better than Greg. If she were with a black man our families would have more in common."

"This isn't London's first marriage. Troy was black, but they didn't work out."

"Troy was a loser. London got with him to piss my parents' off."

"There were others also, Logan."

"I know, but I just can't see our families ever getting along."

"Logan, you have to come to terms with what most of your family is telling you. Let me ask you a question. I know you are close to your mom. Is the way she feels about the Gordons affecting the way you feel about them?"

"I don't think so. I just feel that one day Gracey is going to let Naomi down and that Greg is going to hurt London again."

"Logan, you and Naomi have come a long way. You never thought she would forgive you for the past, but she did. She knows how much you have changed. She feels the same way about Gracey."

"Pastor. I appreciate you taking extra time with me. I want to go talk to my dad then have a long overdue meeting with Simon."

"I think that is a great idea. Clear your head and your heart, Logan. Know that letting the Gordons back into your life doesn't mean you have to totally accept the actions of their past."

"I'm beginning to realize that Pastor. I can't continue to be at odds with my family, especially Naomi. We have fought so hard to be together. I would be lost without her in my life."

"You've taken the first step by admitting there is a problem. Your family and friends love you, Logan. Let them in so they can help you through your difficult time.:

"I will Pastor. Can you say a special prayer for me before I leave?"

"Sure son. Lord of Heaven, I rest underneath your mighty wings of love. I dwell within your gentle heart. I know there is healing in your touch. Through the sufferings of Christ, I can ask of restoration and trust in your goodness. You are my Lord, my Savior. In Jesus name amen." Pastor Sanders watched Logan walk out the door. He hoped the young man could find peace of mind, body, and soul.

Chapter Thirty

Gracey waited in her kitchen for Simon to arrive. They had a lot to talk about. She wanted their relationship to continue, so she knew they had to get on the same page about certain issues. It was important to her that Simon and Logan get back on track. They had been friends forever, so she didn't want them to fall out over her. She also planned to tell Simon they need to let Colby know about their relationship before they went public. Gracey knew that Naomi and Colby had their differences, but they were family. If Colby was hurting Naomi was hurting. Hearing the doorbell, Gracey came out of her thoughts to answer it. She didn't know why but suddenly she was nervous.

"Hi, Simon. Come on in. We can talk in the kitchen." Gracey said.

"Hi sweety." Simon said slightly kissing Gracey on her lips.

"I'm glad you could come over on short notice."

"It's all good. I was free until I meet with Logan later this evening."

"Oh, that's great. That was one of the things I wanted to talk to you about."

"Sweety, I know you're still upset that I told Logan, but he had to know. I love him like a brother. I'm used to sharing my life with him."

"What's done is done. I had an interesting conversation with Logan last night."

"Really."

"Yes. We broke away from the others to have a one-on-one. I finally worked up the nerve to tell him what was really going one with his not accepting me and Greg."

"What might that be?"

"Logan has a problem with me and Greg because we're white."

"Naw that's not true. We have white friends."

"It's not the same when white people join the family."

"What did he have to say?"

"That I was wrong and that I will eventually hurt Naomi."

"I would know if that was the real problem, sweety."

"Things went a little more smoothly after our talk."

"That's cool. Was there another reason you wanted me to come over?"

"Yes. You're right that we need to come clean about our relationship but there is one more issue to tackle."

"And that is?"

"Colby."

"What about Colby?"

"You need to let her know we are dating before she finds out another way."

"I don't think that is necessary."

"Sorry, Simon, but I do think it is necessary. Naomi tells me she isn't happy about the breakup. I don't want to have any problems down the line that could bring stress to my friendship with Naomi."

"She can be unreasonable at times. I don't want to give her any false notions. The last time we met I told her we should steer clear of each other as much as possible."

"Simon if your breakup were with someone that wasn't connected to the family it wouldn't be a problem. For me to stay on a positive path, I have to be proactive about possible stressful situations."

"Well, I guess we could…" Simon stopped what he was saying when Gracey's doorbell rang.

Gracey excuse herself to answer the door. To her surprise an angry Colby was on the other side.

"What are you doing here, Colby?" Gracey asked.

"Where the hell is, he?" Colby pushed her way in searching Gracey's condo."

"What are you doing here, Colby?" Simon asked Colby as he came out of the kitchen.

"I know this better not be who you dumped me for, Simon."

"Colby, we ended our relationship because it wasn't working any longer." Simon explained.

"We didn't end it you ended it, Simon."

"You shouldn't be here, Colby. You need to leave." Simon said.

"You can't tell me what I need to do. I knew something was fishy about the two of you."

"Colby this is between you and Simon." Gracey said leaving the room.

"That's right traitor. Run away like a coward." Colby yelled as Graccy left the room.

When Naomi received the stressing call from Gracey, she had a feeling that would happen. Colby wasn't finished with Simon. Naomi was glad that London and Greg were still at their house when Gracey called. Greg wanted to go over to Gracey's house with Naomi and Logan, but Naomi wanted him to stay with London and the children. When Naomi and Logan pulled up at Gracey's condo she could hear Colby yelling at Simon. A nervous Gracey answered the door.

"I'm so sorry to bother you guys. I just didn't know what to do. Colby refuses to leave." Gracey said.

"Oh Lord. Here comes another traitor. Did you know that Simon dumped me for this trick?" Colby said angerly at Naomi.

"Cob, you shouldn't be here." Naomi said shortening Colby's name.

"I take that as a yes. How could you do this to me, Naomi. You know how much I love Simon."

"I didn't do anything to you, Colby. It wasn't my place to tell you."

"Another cop out. You always get on your self-righteous kick when you don't want to deal with reality."

"You need to watch yourself, Colby." Logan said. Not liking the way Colby was talking to his wife.

"Don't you talk to me, Logan. Naomi should have never gotten back with your lying cheating behind. Now she wants to bring another screwed up family into our lives."

"Let's go, Colby." Simon said sternly.

"I'm not going anywhere with you." Colby replied.

"Cob, you're making this situation worse. I'll follow you home so we can talk."

"I don't want to talk to you, Naomi. You should have told me about this. I don't trust anything you have to say to me."

"You need to go or I'm going to call the police." Gracey threaten.

Before anyone could stop her Colby cross the room then slapped Gracey so hard she felled to the floor. "I wish you would do something like that, heifer."

Logan and Simon grabbed Colby and ushered her to the door. Naomi followed behind because she didn't want Colby to get hurt. "I'm driving you home, Colby. Logan when you are done here you can head home. I'll have mom or dad to drop me back off at home."

Logan and Simon put Colby in the passenger side of her car. Simon ran back into the house to check on Gracey. Logan gave his wife a kiss and told her to be careful. When Logan went back into Gracey's house she was sitting on her living room sofa with Simon. Tears were rolling down her face.

"Logan, I'm so sorry this happened. I just wanted Colby to leave."

"Don't' worry about it. Naomi and her parents will deal with Colby.

"I'm going to call it a night. I know you guys were supposed to meet up later. Just stay here to have your talk. There is plenty of food if you want to make yourselves something to eat." Gracey left the room. She was afraid something like this would happen. She didn't want to have a setback, but this was too much for her to deal with. She couldn't wait for her appointment Monday with Dr. Burbank. Maybe he was right, and she was moving too fast.

Unbreakable: Gracey's Redemption

Epilogue

Thanksgiving Day

A lot had changed over the last few months. Gracey felt so blessed that her job still brought her so much joy. Going back to school was tough, but Simon was right there to root her on. Their relationship had changed a lot since the incident at her condo with Colby. They were with each other almost every day. Their bond was a blessing in so many ways. She finally listened to Dr. Burbank and stop putting so much significance in her friendship with Naomi. He made her see that she was holding on to her friendship with Naomi as a lifeline.

It took a few months, but Colby finally apologized to everyone for her irrational behavior. At the many family gatherings since that day, they all managed to get along. The biggest change in relationship was with Logan. He finally seemed to come to terms with whatever problem he had with her family. The three families have learned to bridge their gap and show a united front for the children. It was a miracle that the parents now enjoyed being together. There wasn't a fuss when Gloria offered to hold Thanksgiving dinner at her house. The mothers worked on the menu together. Now as they all sat around the huge table Gracey wanted to start the conversation.

"I can't believe this day has happened. To see all three families in the same room without tearing each other apart is a blessing from God. I think it will be a good idea to have a representative from each family to say what they are thankful for." Gracey sat back down then nodded to her dad.

"Looking around this room I see hope for the future. To watch my daughter become a self-sufficient young woman is a true blessing. As for my eldest son words cannot express the joy it brings to this family that you have made a family with the woman that is such a big part of your heart. Glenn your mom and I would like to say we are sorry. Greg and Gracey has been such a big part of our lives that sometimes we forgot that you need us too. To the Lewis and Nichols families, thank you all for allowing our family to be a part of your family." Greg Sr. sat down so Logan Sr could take the floor next.

"Our families have been through a lot of ups and downs. I didn't think we would ever be on the same page. The main thing I'm so proud of all of us for is that we put the children first. Our lives will forever be intertwined. Logan, my son. I'm so proud that you faced your issues head on. Men sometime let their pride rule their lives. You hung in there and for that you will always be blessed. To my baby girl. I watched you go from an overactive toddler, to a misguided teenager to a loving mom and supportive wife. Your mom and I are so proud of both of you." With tears in his eyes Logan Sr took his seat so that Naomi's dad could have his turn to speak.

"It's hard to follow those speeches, but I would like to tell my eldest daughter you rock." Everyone at the table laughed at Nelson using such a hip word. I love you to death but this last month since you moved out has been like paradise. London thank you for the bottom of my heart for subletting your condo to Colby. Her mom is still sad to see her go but it's for the best. Naomi, you are the glue that has held all our families together. As we sit here today it's time for you to pass the baton. Focus on you and your family and let the rest take care of itself." Nelson sat down. Then Greg stood.

"I just want to say something briefly. Naomi thank you so much for being the go between when London and I were having issues. Gracey, I can't believe how far you have come. I was so afraid to let you back into my life. Now you are a bright light that will connect us together forever."

My turn Logan said. "Gracey thank you for giving me the push needed to do deal with my inner demons. To my wife. Words cannot express what you mean to me. To say that you are a good wife, mother, friend, attorney is an understatement. Thank you for knowing what I need better that I do."

"Okay I think it's time to wrap this up. Thank you all for your precious speeches. I…"

"One more thing needs to be said." Simon didn't want to be left out. Gracey was caught off guard because she didn't expect Simon to say anything. Simon stood then went to the head of the table where Gracey's parents were sitting. "Mr. and Mrs. Gordon, will you give me the pleasure of allowing me to have your daughter's hand in marriage." Before the Gordons could say anything, Simon went back to his seat where he was sitting next to Gracey. On bended knee he said, "Gracey Gordon will you make me the happiest man alive by accepting this ring in marriage?"

Gracey was speechless. Tears started rolling down her face. She couldn't talk but she shook her head saying yes to Simon's proposal. Everyone in the room even Colby stood and clapped for the newly engaged couple. They all sat down to eat once the commotion was over. There were more toasts here and there but all Gracey could do was stare at the beautiful ring that Simon put on her finger. She lost her appetite for food. All she wanted to do was leave her parents house and spend some alone time with Simon. Looking at the people around the table enjoying their food and conversation make Gracey so happy she didn't know how to put it into words.

As the families started to break up to go home Gracey and Simon stayed behind to spend more time with her parents and Glenn. Greg went home with London, but that was okay because she wasn't planning on staying too long anyway. For the first time since she was a little girl she looked into her mom's eyes and saw love there. Their relationship had been so strained to the point where she thought her mom hated her. Then there was Glenn. They had never gotten along but to see admiration in his eyes, and to see her little brother growing into a responsible young man before her eyes made Gracey sad that she didn't take the time to get to know him better years ago.

She and Simon headed for her condo. Sitting next to him as he drove her home a thousand things went through her head like where they were going to live. Simon had a big four-bedroom house his parents left him when they died so she figured they would live there once her condo lease was up. The final thing that crossed her mind before she dosed off was that maybe she should start a diary about her messed up early life. In all caps the title would read: ***GRACEY'S REDEMPTION.***

Diana Carter

Unbreakable: Gracey's Redemption Discussion Questions

Listed below are discussion questions your book club may be interested in discussing:

1) What comes to your mind when you read about Gracey?

2) Do you think Gracey was putting her recovery in jeopardy by not listening to her therapist?

3) Do you feel that Gracey was fixated on Naomi?

4) Why do you think Logan had such a hard time forgiving the Gordons?

5) Do you feel Naomi was wrong to help Gracey since it bothered Logan so much?

6) Do you think Naomi was right to work with Pastor Sanders to bridge the gaps between the families?

7) Was Colby out of line to go visit Gracey to warn her not to hurt Naomi again?

8) Do you think Logan and Greg bond is strong enough for them to reunite?

9) Was it a good idea for Gracey to date someone from work? Especially Simon?

10) Do you think Naomi was wrong for not telling Colby about Gracey and Simon's relationship?

11) Which character should be the main character if there was a book four?

12) Do you feel Gracey redeemed herself from past sins?

Dear Reader,

I hope you enjoyed reading *Unbreakable: Gracey's Redemption.* This is the third book in the *Unbreakable* romance series. I like to keep my readers entertained by writing something that is satisfying and inspirational. Thank you for taking the time out to read this book.

It would be greatly appreciated if you would consider writing a review of this title on Amazon, Barnes & Noble, and/or the author's website at dianacarterwriter.com in the Comments section under Contact Us (located under the More tab). When you visit the website, you will be informed about upcoming events, publishing services offered, and more.

God's blessings,

Diana Carter

You can find me on the web:

Website: www.dianacarterwriter.com
Amazon Author Page: www.amazon.com/author/diana.carter
Goodreads: www.Goodreads.com/dianacarter

Diana Carter

Author's Information

Diana Carter started her writing career after taking a personality test many years ago and disagreeing with the results. After talking to the administrator of that test, Diana was encouraged to submit the book she had written for publication. Born was her first book ***Broken Promises: Shattered Dreams*** which was published on April 10, 2014 by Outskirts Press. This title was later republished by Diana's publishing company, Let's Do This Publishing, LLC (LDTP) in 2019. Along with the first book in the ***Broken Promises*** series, books two and three and the first book in the ***Dark Revenge*** series were also republished by LDTP. See the list of other titles written by Diana in the front of this book.

Diana has a passion for writing fictional stories that will not only entertain her readers but also have a lasting impact. She loves to write and looks forward to continuing for many years to come. When she takes a break from writing, she likes to spend time with her children, grandchildren, bowl, read, and tutoring disadvantaged adults.

You can find additional information on Diana's website at www.dianacarterwriter.com, or by checking out her Amazon page at: amazon.com/author/diana.carter or if you like to personally reach her do so via email at diana.carter44@gmail.com.

www.ingramcontent.com/pod-product-compliance
Lightning Source LLC
Chambersburg PA
CBHW031120080526
44587CB00011B/1045